Praise for

Deborah Carlisle Solomon's

Baby Knows Best

"One of the best things that ever happened to me as a mother was discovering RIE. I'm forever indebted to Deborah Solomon and my other RIE teachers for helping me slow down, understand, and respect my baby. Even though my daughter is now nine, she is still a RIE baby at heart: calm, confident, and self-motivated. *Baby Knows Best* is a treasure of insights and wisdom. I will be giving this invaluable book to every new mother I know."

—Maria Semple, author of *Where'd You Go, Bernadette*

"Outstanding! Deborah Solomon did it! She brought Magda Gerber to life in this absorbing and powerful book full of Gerber's words and ideas! Reading it took me back to the 1970s, when I sat on the floor and watched this famous infant expert in action working with a group of babies and parents. Deborah Solomon's own experiences augment Magda's teachings and expand our thinking about who babies are and what they need. For many readers this book is bound to be loaded with potent new ideas—ideas that in some ways are quite different from the usual advice experts give parents. Easy to read, eye-opening, hard to forget!"

—Janet Gonzalez-Mena, coauthor of *Infants, Toddlers, and Caregivers* and author of *Diversity in Early Care and Education: Honoring Differences*

"The RIE program is the single most relatable, intuitive, and commonsense approach to the modern-day conundrum of parenting. *Baby Knows Best* is the guidebook. It helps you get back to basics and makes you a better, more confident parent as you learn that Babies do indeed Know Best. A must-have on yours and your baby's library shelf."　　—Jamie Lee Curtis

"RIE gave us a loving methodology for how to do the most important thing in the world—understand and nurture our babies. It fostered a communication and interplay that we've built upon all their lives. This was invaluable and loving knowledge."　　—Jason Alexander

"I think RIE should be a national program so that parents all over the country can have the opportunity that my family had."
　　—Dee Dee Myers, former White House press secretary

"RIE has been a blessing in our lives, giving us the chance to learn that our baby can teach us best when we observe carefully. We've learned to respect him as he expresses his needs."
　　—Gustavo Dudamel, music director of the Los Angeles Philharmonic, and his wife, Eloísa Maturén

"My greatest fear as a parent was making mistakes. I wanted some kind of rule book that told me how to handle every situation with an infant. RIE is the closest thing that I have found to this 'holy grail.' How to be attentive but not intrusive, loving but not smothering, kind but not indulging, guiding but not controlling, strict but not rigid—all this wonderfully laid out in RIE's Educaring Approach. We are raising an independent being that I can feel incredibly close to. Thank you, Magda Gerber and all the wonderful infant Educarers!"
　　—Hank Azaria

"This book will be an invaluable contribution for parents and for anybody who cares about young children. RIE is a pioneering approach to caregiving that anticipated what science now tells us: that babies and young children thrive with sensitive care that is responsive to their signals and developmental needs. For parents who often feel torn between multiple demands, RIE offers a gentle, supportive approach that fosters their self-confidence and helps them rediscover the joys of raising a child. The RIE approach is a refreshing departure from the didactic, overly prescriptive books that seem to dominate the parenting literature. I strongly recommend this book."

—Alicia F. Lieberman, PhD, author of
The Emotional Life of the Toddler

"This terrific book is written by someone who really understands daily life with a baby. Deborah Carlisle Solomon shows how you can build an enjoyable relationship with your baby through the power of observation."

—Sue Gerhardt, author of *Why Love Matters*

"A quietly brilliant parenting book, full of wisdom and calm guidance." —*Publishers Weekly* (starred review)

BABY KNOWS BEST

Raising a Confident and Resourceful Child, the RIE® Way

Deborah Carlisle Solomon

Photographs by Barrow Davis-Tolot

LITTLE, BROWN AND COMPANY

New York Boston London

Little, Brown and Company
Hachette Book Group
1290 Avenue of the Americas, New York, NY 10104
littlebrown.com

Originally published in hardcover by Little, Brown and Company, December 2013
First Little, Brown trade paperback edition, January 2015

Little, Brown and Company is a division of Hachette Book Group, Inc. The Little, Brown name and logo are trademarks of Hachette Book Group, Inc.

All photographs are by Barrow Davis-Tolot, except for the photograph on page 8 of Magda Gerber, which is by Imre Gerber, and the one on page 217, by Elio Tolot. Photos edited by Barrow Davis-Tolot.

The publisher is not responsible for websites (or their content) that are not owned by the publisher.

RIE, Educaring, the Educaring Approach, Educarer, RIE Associate, RIE Parent-Infant Guidance, RIE Foundations, RIE Practicum, RIE Internship, RIE Mentor, RIE Certified Program, Before Baby, Nurturing Nanny, Cuidadoras Cariñosas, and additional marks are trademarks owned by Resources for Infant Educarers (www.rie.org).

The Hachette Speakers Bureau provides a wide range of authors for speaking events. To find out more, go to hachettespeakersbureau.com or call (866) 376-6591.

Library of Congress Cataloging-in-Publication Data
Solomon, Deborah Carlisle.
    Baby knows best : raising a confident and resourceful child, the RIE™ Way / Deborah Carlisle Solomon ; photographs by Barrow Davis-Tolot.—First edition.
        pages cm
    Includes bibliographical references and index.
    ISBN 978-0-316-21920-4 (hc) / 978-0-316-21919-8 (pb)
    1. Gifted children.   2. Gifted children—Family relationships.
3. Achievement motivation in children.   4. Parenting.   I. Title.
    HQ773.5.S65 2013
    305.9'089083—dc23   2013025868

10 9 8 7 6 5 4 3 2 1

RRD-C

Printed in the United States of America

*This book is dedicated to Magda Gerber,
to RIE Associates who share her
important work with others,
and to the parents and caregivers who
practice her Educaring Approach.*

Contents

BABY
KNOWS
BEST

Introduction

Observe more, do less.

—Magda Gerber, *Dear Parent*

Parenting is a difficult job and one that is impossible to fully prepare for. My son's newborn diapers were neatly stacked, the drawer was full of Onesies, and my heart was full of love for a child I had yet to meet. Then Elijah was born. I asked the nurse at the hospital if I could stay just one more night. I had spent so much time lying awake gazing at my baby that I was utterly exhausted. The nurses kept saying, "You need to sleep when he sleeps," but I didn't want to rest. I wanted to observe his every move and respond to his every gurgle. We arrived home, and the constant caring for my son hit me like a ton of bricks. I had never had a full-time job that was so, literally, full-time. Or one that was so demanding as well as important to me. When my husband and I took Elijah for his one-month checkup, his pediatrician asked me if I had been out of the house. When I told him that I hadn't even taken a walk in the neighborhood, he ordered me to stop hibernating and get out of the house. But how would I do that? Days went by when I couldn't even manage to squeeze in a shower. In those early weeks, having it sufficiently together to go for a stroll in the neighborhood seemed like climbing Everest. What if we were out and he started to cry? What if he was too cold? Too warm? What if it started to rain? What if...? I had to be prepared for any contingency, didn't I? It wasn't that I was particularly anxious, but I felt I had to have all the answers.

In those first weeks, I experienced a potent combination of exhilaration and exhaustion. I was certainly elated to be a mother, but because I was working so hard at it, some of the pure pleasure of parenting was lost. When Elijah made the slightest peep, I leaped up to see what was the matter. His cries, whether big or small, meant there was something I needed to fix, and the sooner the better. Responding so quickly to my son's upset made it impossible for me to pull back and consider the full picture. I was operating under the assumption that babies should be happy all the time. I don't know anyone who is happy *all* the time, so why was I expecting something different from my baby?

When Elijah was a year old, I was fortunate to discover the work of Magda Gerber, through her book *Your Self-Confident Baby*. The title intrigued me because self-confidence was not something I would ever have ascribed to a baby. I read the book, and my husband, Jonny, and I found our way to RIE Parent-Infant Guidance classes, which had a profound impact on the way we parent and our relationship with our son. Over time I slowed down, learned to observe, and discovered just how competent and capable Elijah could be. Once I got to know my son not as "a baby" but as a unique individual, our interactions fundamentally changed. I relaxed, my confidence grew, and being with Elijah became a lot more fun.

You may have been parented in a way that you would like to emulate with your child. Or you may want to parent very differently from the way you were parented, to let go of patterns from your childhood that you would prefer not to repeat. But how do you break a cycle that has been passed down from one generation to the next? Awareness and intention are important first steps, but then what? How do you replace what you know with what you don't know?

For most of us, parenting is the most important job we will

have in our lives, and yet it is often one we are unprepared for—at least in the way of a formal education. While biology is part of the standard high school curriculum, basic infant development is nowhere to be found. Parents who consider themselves competent in other areas of their lives sometimes feel unsure when it comes to caring for their babies. They presume they can rely on instinct but find themselves confused about how best to care for their baby. This is compounded by the fact that little or no social service support exists for new parents in most communities, and many new parents live miles away from their own parents or other family members who might offer guidance and support. No wonder many new parents go to the bookstore or search the Internet in the middle of the night to find answers to an immediate challenge. But it can be confusing when one answer entirely contradicts another. What's a parent to do?

The Educaring® Approach is the basis for this book and provides a framework and practical tools that will support you in finding your own solutions to all sorts of parenting challenges and in becoming a more confident parent. The approach is based on the unique principles and revolutionary teachings of Magda Gerber, world-renowned founder of RIE® (Resources for Infant Educarers). A comprehensive approach to caring for and being with your baby, Educaring lays the foundation for a lifelong relationship based on respect. It shows you ways to understand what your baby really needs, and teaches you how to respond to those needs accurately. Although the approach focuses on newborns to two-year-olds, the concepts will continue to serve you well long after your baby is out of diapers. No special equipment is necessary. All that is needed is an open mind and heart.

ABOUT MAGDA GERBER

Magda Gerber was born in Budapest, Hungary. She married at eighteen and shortly thereafter became a mother. She remarked that although she was well educated, nothing in her studies had prepared her for being a parent. One day, one of Magda's daughters, who was then four years old, was sick and needed medical attention. The family pediatrician was unavailable, so Magda's daughter suggested they call the mother of one of her friends, who was a pediatrician. Dr. Emmi Pikler came to see Magda's daughter at their home and inquired about her sore throat. When Magda began to speak on her daughter's behalf, Dr. Pikler gestured for Magda to be quiet so that the child could respond. Magda was astonished by her daughter's ability to clearly articulate how she was feeling. Dr. Pikler asked permission of Magda's daughter before looking in her throat, and Magda was stunned by the cooperative exchange between them. The interaction not only revealed to Magda her daughter's competence but astounded her with its respectful give-and-take. From then on, Dr. Pikler was the pediatrician to Magda's children, and thus began a long collaboration and friendship that continued until Emmi Pikler's death in 1984.

When World War II ended, the Hungarian government commissioned Dr. Pikler to establish a residential facility to care for children from birth to three years of age who had been orphaned during the war or whose parents were unable to care for them. Six months after she received the commission, the National Methodological Institute for Infant Care and Education was opened. Here, all those who cared for the children followed Dr. Pikler's very specific pedagogy. It was a vastly different place from other residential facilities where babies, at best, had their basic needs attended to or, at worst, were victims of indifferent treatment and "warehousing." The orphanage was commonly referred to as "Lóczy," for the street on which it was located, and upon Dr. Pikler's death, it was renamed the Pikler Institute in her honor. The institute cared for children for over sixty years, and although it is no longer a residential facility, it continues to be an international beacon of quality infant care and education. Among other things, Dr. Pikler is well known for her research about and approach to *natural* gross motor development, which was quite controversial at a time when many in the medical community were espousing the benefits of stimulation to teach babies how to move.

Magda studied with Dr. Pikler at Lóczy and went on to earn her master's degree in early childhood education in Budapest. She and her family left Hungary in 1956 after the revolution and immigrated to the United States the following year. They first settled in Boston, where Magda worked as an interpreter at Harvard University. A year later, the family made its way to Los Angeles, where Magda worked with children with cerebral palsy at Children's Hospital and then with children with autism spectrum disorders at the Dubnoff School. She applied the principles she learned at Lóczy and added her own insights, gathered through her unique educational and professional experiences. She had the ability to see the universality in all of us and applied the same principles with all children, including those with special needs. As Magda said, "My magic was simply observing closely and expecting of the children only what they could do. When a child is expected to do something he cannot, he is set up for failure."[1] Those who knew Magda describe her extraordinary empathy and instinctive ability to relate to people. Magda had such compassion for the tender and vulnerable new parents who found their way to her classes, and she was able to gently guide them without undermining their confidence.

In 1972, Stanford pediatric neurologist Tom Forrest invited Magda to join him as founding codirector of the Demonstration Infant Program (DIP), a preventive mental health project commissioned by the Children's Health Council of Palo Alto, California. The following year, Magda began teaching parent-infant guidance classes in Los Angeles and in 1978, with Dr. Forrest, founded Resources for Infant Educarers (RIE), based in Los Angeles. At RIE, Magda taught an innovative kind of parent-infant class where parents were encouraged to observe their babies as they played freely, as an RIE facilitator modeled when and how to intervene with the babies. Since those early days, thousands of parents and caregivers have studied at RIE, and tens of thousands of babies have been cared for by adults who practice the Educaring Approach. Magda died in 2007, but her important work continues around the world through the dedicated RIE Associates who conduct classes for parents and professionals, as well as those who work directly with babies and toddlers.

Magda said she felt so fortunate to receive such valuable guidance from Dr. Pikler that she was compelled to share it with others. Her passion and life's work were helping parents and caregivers to understand babies and to learn what it means to interact with them respectfully. She taught that babies come into the world as complete human beings with their own distinct points of view. She helped us to see that by slowing down, observing, and taking the time to wait, we could understand our babies better and respond to their needs more accurately. She showed us what it means to *respect* a baby while also respecting ourselves.

Magda came from a European perspective, and this is reflected in her Educaring Approach. Even if you come from a similar cultural background, you may find that some of what you read here may differ from your cultural or family practices. Although habits and customs may vary from culture to culture, and different families certainly have their own unique way of doing things, I believe that the Educaring Approach can help any parent to better understand his or her baby and make the role of parent easier and more enjoyable. The essential truths of the Educaring Approach can be beneficial and relevant to all kinds of families, whether they consist of a single parent, a mother and father, two moms, two dads, or extended families with grandparents who take an active role in caring for the baby.

I hope you will use *Baby Knows Best* as a guidebook. Each chapter begins with a relevant quote from Magda. In the next chapter, you will be introduced to basic RIE principles and concepts that form the foundation of the approach. Later chapters address specific topics and issues that are part of everyday life with a baby or toddler and suggest ways of handling them. Throughout the book, parents as well as RIE educators offer their thoughts and insights on the Educaring Approach. Gender is referred to as she/her and he/his in alternate chapters. You will note that specific ages are not implied for major milestones such as rolling over, sitting up, crawling, and walking. Magda did not like to attach ages to these events because she wanted to encourage parents to appreciate what their baby was doing rather than measuring and comparing him to the supposed norm.

If you read this book and decide that you would like to make some changes in the way you care for your baby, I suggest that you start with just one or two RIE principles or ideas and practice them for a while until you and your baby become comfortable with them. Doing a lot of things differently, all at once, may be overwhelming for you and confusing for your baby, so take your time. There's no hurry. After all, this is the beginning of a lifelong relationship.

I hope you will discover, as I did, how the Educaring Approach can help you get to know your baby better, become a more confident parent, and find more joy in parenting. It can be a parent's greatest pleasure to witness a baby's growing competence, self-reliance, and resourcefulness. It is an extraordinary gift to have a respectful, cooperative, intimate, and loving relationship with your child.

1. The RIE Way

Our goal is to help parents learn to live and let live with their infants and later with their older children. Such insight cannot be "taught." Long-term learning is a slow process. It must happen organically — allowing for time in which the seeds of understanding may sprout, grow, bloom, and bear fruit.
—Magda Gerber, *Dear Parent*

Enter an RIE Parent-Infant Guidance class or the home of an RIE family, and you'll find a gated-off area that has been created as a safe space for the babies to play. For young babies, a thin, firm mat made of foam, covered with a cotton sheet, has been placed on top of the floor or rug to ensure a safe and clean play surface. It's a no-shoes area for both adults and babies.

At RIE Parent-Infant Guidance classes, parents sit around the perimeter of the room on small cushions or BackJack floor chairs with their babies in their laps. When parents and babies first arrive in class, they take the time to "warm in," or transition, to being in the gated-off play space together. The parents quietly talk about their week and may ask the RIE facilitator for guidance on issues that came up at home since the last class. When a baby shows interest in being on the mat to be near the other babies and play objects, his parent lays him on his back on the mat, or he moves toward the floor on his own to explore.

The play objects arranged around the room are simple; they don't have busy patterns or shiny sparkles. You won't see the latest faddish toys that promise to be entertaining and educational. The objects don't light up. They don't make sounds, unless a baby hits the object on the floor or against another object. To an adult, the play objects may look downright boring. And aren't some of those objects—measuring cups and colanders—from the kitchen cupboard?

For young babies, there are tented cotton napkins and just a few objects of various materials to mouth and chew on, such as metal frozen-juice lids, silicone pot holders, and wooden rings. For crawling babies, there are additional objects such as cups made of wood, metal, and plastic, or balls that are bumpy or smooth and made of cotton, rubber, or plastic. For toddlers, who often like to collect and sort things, there are also buckets and bowls.

After the warming-in period, the RIE facilitator asks the adults to sit without talking for a period of quiet observation. Except for the sounds of babies gurgling, cooing, and babbling, their sounds of exertion and effort, and the possible clatter of objects, the room is quiet as the adults observe the children for twenty minutes or so. They observe as six-month-old Eli crawls across the room to reach a plastic colander full of balls. As Adrianna lies on her back, mouthing a wooden ring, Aidan scoots over and takes it from her. Across the mat, Miles and Keesha are sitting up, facing each other. Miles picks up a small metal cup, and for a while he and Keesha pass it back and forth between them. Then Miles taps the cup against Keesha's head, and she immediately begins to cry. Parents stay seated while the facilitator moves close to the babies and says to Miles, "Keesha's upset. If you want to bang the cup, you can bang it on the floor." She gently strokes each child's head, saying, "Gently. Softly."

When the structured observation time is up, the facilitator may ask, "What did you observe about your baby or someone else's baby? What did you observe about yourself?"

Eli's dad says, "Eli spotted the colander all the way across the room and worked hard to get to it. He was so pleased when he got there and finally had it in his hands. I have to work on my own impatience because sometimes I just want to hand things to him."

Adrianna's mom says, "When Adrianna was lying on her

back, playing with the ring, I was anxious when Aidan crawled over to her. But then I noticed that she didn't seem to mind at all, and when he took the ring from her, she just looked around for something else to play with. That surprised me."

Miles's mom says, "When you moved in close and said, 'Keesha's upset,' Miles really seemed to listen. You brought a peaceful presence that helped both children to calm." Keesha's mom says, "My first instinct was to come close to comfort Keesha. But she didn't even look to me. You gave her what she needed."

Observation is an art form. It's not something that most people can do easily, but when they're encouraged to do it, they learn to let go and enjoy it. Parents can begin to relax and see who their child is becoming instead of thinking they need to be the cause of, or catalyst for, their child's development. Observation is a win-win situation because it's liberating for the parent and it's liberating for the child as well. People come to RIE because they're intrigued by having seen a child who is more independent, more calmly conducting herself in the world, and they wonder, "What is this?" Given the chance to live with a child whom they could like a lot, they grab on to it. Doing less is the cheese at the end of the tunnel. After her husband attended an RIE class, one woman said, "What did you do to my husband? He's a changed man."

— Elizabeth Memel, RIE Associate

In Parent-Infant Guidance classes, parents observe their babies, come to appreciate all that their babies are doing, and trust in their baby's individual timetable for achieving milestones. By learning to hold back rather than quickly intervening to rescue or problem-solve for their babies, parents are often surprised to see just how competent their babies can be. Over time and with practice, parents become more confident in their parenting skills, and the babies become confident, self-reliant, and resourceful, as both take pleasure in just being together without any sort of agenda.

When my wife, Natascha, told me about RIE, I said, "Wait, you want me to pay money to sit in a room with other parents and babies and watch Billy crawl around? I can do that at home!" But then I really learned to stop and observe.

— Jeremy Aldridge

ATTACHMENT THEORY

Attachment or *attachment theory* refers to the developing connection between a baby and the significant other who cares for him—most often his mother or father. The nature of the attachment relationship is largely formed by the sensitive responsiveness of the parent to the baby and the overall quality of the baby-parent interactions. In secure attachment, the parent helps the baby learn to self-soothe and also encourages and takes pleasure in the baby's independent exploration. Learning when to hold close and when to let go is a skill that parents are called on to employ throughout their child's life. Magda's genius was in helping us to see the world from the baby's point of view and showing us practical ways to respond to babies with care and respect.

THE EDUCARING APPROACH

Magda Gerber said that "we should educate while we care and care while we educate" and coined the terms *Educarer* and *Educaring* to describe the ways in which caring and educating are intertwined.[1] She taught that the intimate caregiving activities of diapering, dressing, bathing, and feeding are not only relationship-building opportunities but also opportunities for learning. Her approach is based on a set of basic RIE principles that inform all parent-child interactions.

RIE Principles

In addition to respect and authenticity, seven basic RIE principles form the foundation of the Educaring Approach. They are introduced in this chapter and expanded on in greater detail throughout the book. These are not a rigid set of principles that must be doggedly enforced and followed but rather can serve as guideposts to support you in building a respectful relationship with your baby. These principles will help you respond confidently to the inevitable parenting challenges that will arise. Parents who practice the Educaring Approach discover how flexible it is and often remark that it makes parenting easier and more enjoyable. The Educaring Approach guides parents to create a more harmonious and peaceful life at home with their babies. And who doesn't want that? Here are the RIE principles, exactly as Magda wrote them.

1. Basic trust in the child to be an initiator, an explorer, and a self-learner

"An infant always learns. The less we interfere with the natural process of learning, the more we can observe how much infants learn all the time."[2]

When you trust in your baby's competence, you can relax, secure in the knowledge that he will let you know when he needs you and that you don't have to push, prod, or teach him for him to develop fully, happily, and well. This kind of trust develops over time, as you observe your baby to get to know him better, understand his cues, and notice what interests him. All babies are naturally curious and motivated from within. They don't need us to instruct or teach them. Give your baby the opportunity to discover and try things out on his own and allow him the time he needs to develop at his own pace. There may be times when you feel impatient or anxious, but trusting in your baby's unique developmental timetable will serve you both well.

2. An environment for the child that is physically safe, cognitively challenging, and emotionally nurturing

"Contrary to what many people believe, a gated room is a safe room which gives infants freedom *to move and explore in safe and familiar surroundings."[3]*

Magda defined a safe space as one that if you got locked out of the house or apartment for many hours, you would return to find your baby hungry, upset, and needing a new diaper but unharmed. A safe play space allows you to fully relax, knowing you don't have to be on guard to ensure your baby's safety. It also gives your baby the freedom to fully explore in his play area, never hearing you say, "Don't touch that. Don't climb on that. That's not safe." Provide a safe space for your baby—a separate room or a gated-off area—with no potential hazards. Get down on your hands and knees and crawl around. Experience the environment from your baby's point of view. Are the bookshelves securely fastened to the wall? Are the outlets covered? Could your baby crawl up onto the sofa and topple off the back? If so, your baby is not safe alone in the space. Make the play area safe so that it works for both of you—so that he can be free to explore, and you can relax knowing there's no potential danger.

A cognitively challenging environment provides opportunities for exploration and learning with developmentally appropriate play objects. A plastic jar with a lid for unscrewing is appropriate for a toddler but will provide too much challenge for a young baby. Balls can be fun for a crawling baby or toddler who can retrieve the ball when it rolls away, but not ideal for a baby who is not yet crawling and does not have the ability to pursue the ball himself.

In an emotionally nurturing environment, your baby can relax and trust that you will be available for emotional support when he needs you. He can enjoy independent exploration and also initiate playful interactions with you as you appreciate and take pleasure in his play.

3. Time for uninterrupted play

> *"The less we interrupt, the more easily infants develop a long attention span."*[4]

All babies know how to play. They don't need us to teach them. It is natural to play with your baby, but let him be the one to initiate the play. Babies can learn to play happily on their own, in their safe play area. When babies are given the opportunity to explore and experiment independently, they discover their own inner resources and what interests them.

When your baby is playing, he's not just fiddling with an object. He is learning about that particular object, making discoveries about cause and effect, and how he can impact the object. Let your baby decide *if* he wants to play (perhaps he'd prefer to lie on his back and watch the dust particles in the sunlight), *when* to play, *what* object to play with, *what* he'd like to do with it, and for *how long*. Giving your baby time for uninterrupted play every day helps to preserve a long attention span that many babies are born with. It also helps to promote concentration, self-reliance, and problem-solving skills.

4. Freedom to explore and interact with other infants

> *"Whereas others often restrict infant-infant interaction (such as infants touching each other) for fear of their hurting one another,* Educarers facilitate interactions by closely observing *in order to know when to intervene and when not to."*[5]

Babies are fascinated by other babies. It's wonderful for your baby to have the opportunity to play and explore with a small and consistent group of babies of his own developmental stage, with you or another attentive adult nearby to provide emotional support and safety.

Your baby will learn about himself and others through interacting with his peers. There will be times when he may choose to sit in your lap and observe the other babies rather than venturing out. At RIE, if a child wants to remain close to his parent for the entire ninety-minute class, that's just fine. There's no agenda stating that he needs to move away from his parent or play with an object. Just as your baby will roll over when he's ready, he'll also indicate when he's ready to move off your lap to explore, without any coaxing or urging from you. Readiness will depend on your baby's temperament and his developmental stage. When he is ready, your baby will engage with objects and other babies in ways that interest him. In the meantime, he may enjoy sitting on your lap, observing the other babies and parents.

5. Involvement of the child in all caregiving activities to allow the child to become an active participant rather than a passive recipient

> *"The natural time to be wholeheartedly with your child is the time you do spend together anyway—while you* care *for your baby. Think of these 'taking-care-of' routines as very special, the 'refueling' time for both of you—time for intimate togetherness."*[6]

Caregiving times are not just about accomplishing a particular task like diapering, bathing, or feeding. They are intimate, relationship-building opportunities that can be pleasurable for both of you. They are activities that you do *with* your baby rather than *to* or *for* your baby. You can invite even the youngest baby to participate in his care. From birth, when you diaper your baby, you can say, "Will you lift your bottom for me?" as you gently touch your newborn's bottom. When that touch and those words are followed by lifting your baby's bottom, he will come to understand their meaning and participate when he is ready. Caregiving times also provide rich opportunities for language learning and offer possibilities for participation, cooperation, and delight. So slow down, take your time, and enjoy these intimate moments together.

6. Sensitive observation of the child in order to understand his or her needs

> *"The more we do, the busier we are, the less we really pay attention."*[7]

By observing your baby, you will come to understand him better and appreciate all that he is doing and learning. The bottle or breast may always quiet his cry, but what if he's not hungry but sleepy instead? Slowing down and taking the time to pause and observe your baby before rushing in can help you to respond more accurately to his needs. You may be thinking, "I never take my eyes off my baby!" But observing is very different from looking and watching. It requires you to quiet yourself, pause, be patient, and try to see your baby as if for the first time. This takes practice because we often see only what we expect to see. By quietly observing your baby—in his crib, in your arms, or while he's playing on the floor—you will get to know him better and appreciate all that he's doing with much more detail.

7. Consistency and clearly defined limits and expectations to develop discipline

> *"A positive goal to strive for when disciplining would be to raise children we not only love, but in whose company we love being."*[8]

Setting limits clearly and following through on them consistently help a child to feel secure because he learns what is expected of him. If you don't want your toddler bouncing on the sofa, let him know and offer an alternative, suggesting something else that he can jump on. Sometimes we have to repeat a limit over and over again until a child finally internalizes the limit and becomes *self-disciplined*. Patience is key. Of course, an authoritarian parent may get the desired result more quickly, but at what cost to the child's sense of self and the parent-child relationship? It is not necessary or wise to punish, chastise, or use time-outs with a baby or toddler who repeatedly tests the limit.

In addition to the basic RIE principles, the following concepts support the Educaring Approach.

Respect

The Educaring Approach is based on *respect*, both for our babies and for ourselves. Most people would agree that it is important to respect one another, but respect means different things to different people. For some, respect is a one-way street where children show respect to their parents and elders but little respect flows in the opposite direction. For me, I feel respected when people give me their full, undivided attention; when they allow me to talk without interrupting and they listen without judgment; when they honor my point of view, even if they disagree with me. I become prickly when I witness hierarchical or patriarchal behavior and when I see people being treated as less than, just because they are younger or are the employee rather than the employer. A key to creating harmonious families and a more peaceful world lies in learning how to interact and coexist with one another respectfully. Children don't learn about this when they begin to walk or when they go to nursery school. They learn about respect at the very beginning of their lives through their interactions with the adults who care for them.

The Educaring Approach teaches us to respect a baby by touching him gently, carrying him securely, and moving slowly. We show respect by always telling him what we're going to do before we do it. "I'm going to pick you up now." "I'm going to the kitchen and will be right back." "Let's take off your diaper now." We look for eye contact with our baby, but we don't force it, respecting his desire and need to look away and turn inward when he needs to. We talk directly to the baby and give him time to take in what we've said. We don't try to distract him from his feelings but allow him to fully express his emotions until he's all done. We don't multitask but rather give him our full, undivided attention during caregiving routines of feeding, diapering, bathing, and dressing, and at other times as well.

We demonstrate *self*-respect by taking care of our own needs so that we can more easily and happily care for our baby. By taking care of our own needs, without guilt, we are setting a good example that our needs and our baby's needs are both important. "I know you want me to stay with you right now, but I need to take a shower. I'll be done in a little while, and then I'll be back." "I love playing with you, but I'm feeling tired. I'm going to lie down in my room for a few minutes while you play."

Authenticity

Authenticity means the genuineness or truth of something. Allowing your baby to be his authentic self requires letting go of preconceived ideas, sitting back to observe and truly see him in the moment, and not assuming he will respond in the way he did yesterday. When you come to your baby with wonder and curiosity, he will often surprise you, and your understanding of him will deepen. Instead of being limited to the role of a cute, cuddly, kissable baby, he will be revealed to you as the complex human being that he truly is. As he grows, your child will learn to find the balance between being true to himself and being a member of a larger social group.

My son taught me valuable lessons about letting go of preconceived ideas and the joy and surprise that comes with being open to possibilities. When Elijah was about three years old, my husband and I got him a toddler-size basketball net. I believe we suffered from the mistaken idea that a boy of his age should start developing his ball skills! But Elijah had an altogether different idea in mind. I watched as he carried his little stool outside and placed it in front of the basketball net. Then he went back inside, retrieved his bin full of small objects, and placed it on the ground next to the stool. He picked up the objects one by one, climbed onto the stool, and dropped them into the net. Some things fell straight through, and others got hung up and had to be disentangled. Some fell quickly and made a loud sound when they dropped, and other, lighter objects took their time and fell soundlessly to the ground. Elijah was gleeful when something fell right through with a thud, and he curiously problem-solved when other objects got caught. He repeated this experiment many times and could be thoroughly involved in it for a half hour or more. Was that what we had expected him to do with the basketball net? No, but it was what captured Elijah's imagination. I have no doubt that, like a scientist, he learned a lot through his experimentation. The basketball net was an important lesson that taught me to let go of any fixed ideas of how I thought Elijah should or would respond—whether to a basketball net or to certain environments or situations. Instead of feeling that I had to lead him or teach him, I learned that the far greater pleasure was to provide a cognitively challenging environment for Elijah and then sit back, relax, and enjoy simply being together as he discovered what interested him.

Slow down.

Do your best never to hurry with your baby. Instead, move slowly. This will help to create a sense of calm and peacefulness. It will give your baby the opportunity to follow what is happening and participate when he is able. How slowly? As slowly as you can. I think of the graceful people who practice tai chi in my neighborhood park. You might think of a movie played in slow motion. Dr. Pikler described it as "ceremonious slowness."[9] Perhaps you have an image from your own experience that will remind you to slow down with your baby.

Narrate and communicate.

You and your baby will convey a lot to each other nonverbally— through your eyes, your touch, your body language and gestures. Although it may seem silly to speak to someone who at first won't understand your words, speaking to your baby about what is happening and what he is experiencing not only is respectful but can help him to make sense of himself and his world. Use words—but not too many—to acknowledge what your baby may be experiencing sensorially. "The washcloth is warm." "I heard the garbage truck." "The light is very bright." "You felt the breeze on your cheek." Use words to acknowledge what your baby might be feeling. When he is upset, narrate what you observe, without making assumptions or judgments. "You're crying really hard. I hear you." If your toddler was holding a ball and is crying because another child took it from him, you can't know for sure if the tears are of frustration, sadness, or anger. You can acknowledge the emotion without defining it specifically by saying something like "Damon has the ball, and you want it, too. You're upset." Using words to mirror your child's emotional state back to him lets him know that he has been seen and understood, and can provide comfort to him.

Do your best to always tell your baby what is about to happen. If you'd like to pick him up, let him know. "I'm going to pick you up now so that we can change your diaper." Then *wait for his response* and move slowly. Not only is this respectful, but he can relax, knowing there will be no surprises. Narrate what you observe or what you are doing together. "You're rubbing your eyes. It looks like you're tired." "Now I'm putting soap on the washcloth." "Let's snap your pajamas."

Be honest with your baby about what you're feeling. This can be beneficial to you by helping to release tension and lay the foundation for a lifetime of open communication. "I'm tired. It's 3:00 a.m., and I want to sleep. I don't know what you need." "You're crying and crying, and I don't know what to do." "I could sit here all day just looking at you. My heart is full. I love you so much."

Magda's lessons about the importance of observation and communication are supported by current research. Arietta Slade, a psychologist at CUNY, says that "it is the mother's observations of the moment to moment changes in the child's mental state, and her representation of these first in gesture and action, and later in words and play, that is at the heart of sensitive caregiving."[10]

The phrases and narrations used throughout the book are not scripts but are merely offered as examples of what you might say in certain situations. Speak naturally to your baby, in a way that is authentic to you.

Establish predictability and routine.

Unlike many adults, who take pleasure in spontaneity and a potentially exciting change of plans, babies enjoy consistency and routine. They like a simple day that is much the same as the one before, where caregiving tasks of diapering, bathing, and feeding happen at an unhurried pace. Simple routines make it possible for a baby to participate more and more and to feel at ease because he comes to know what to anticipate. When days are overscheduled with new people and novel experiences, the unfamiliar can make a baby feel helpless and less than secure. There are times, of course, when small changes happen that upset a baby's equilibrium, even slightly. To mitigate potential upset and to help your baby cope, do your best to tell your baby when a change is about to happen or has happened. "I'm going to the kitchen now." "The door slammed. It made a loud noise." "I'm going to turn off the light."

Allow tarry time.

RIE Associate Diana Suskind coined the term *tarry time* to describe the time given to a baby after he has been told what is about to happen. Slowing down and telling a baby what is about to happen are key, but giving him time to process what has been said and prepare himself is the third part of the equation. When you say, "I'm going to pick you up now," pause and give your baby tarry time to process what you've said. If you wait and observe for several seconds or more, you'll notice when he is ready. He may hold out his arms, lift his shoulders, or kick his legs in excited anticipation of being picked up.

Wants Nothing/Wants Something Time

Magda distinguished quality time into two categories: *wants nothing time* and *wants something time.* During wants nothing time, you have no agenda. You are fully present with your baby, open and available to him. Sit down on the floor in your baby's safe play space, leave your cares and concerns at the door, and just be with your baby. It's a time not to send text messages or read a magazine but to simply enjoy being with your baby, taking your lead from him. If you are in the habit of multitasking or ticking things off a to-do list, wants nothing time may be difficult, particularly in the beginning. I encourage you to persevere. Many parents tell me that wants nothing time is a revelation, and it is a relief to know they don't always have to do something with their babies. If you find yourself being pulled toward your laptop or otherwise distracted, try wants nothing time when you have less on your mind and are able to be fully present.

There are times when you *do* have something to accomplish with your baby or toddler, and these are wants something times—when you want to diaper, dress, feed, or bathe your baby or perhaps buckle him into his car seat. Whereas wants nothing times are free-form and open-ended, wants something times have goals and expectations. "I want to change your diaper." "It's time for your bath." "We need to put on your jacket now." They may involve limit setting and early discipline. "I see you're enjoying splashing in the bath, but it's time to get out of the tub." "I know you don't like the car seat, but I need to buckle you in so we can leave." Acknowledge your child's point of view and invite his cooperation as you kindly and firmly let him know what needs to happen. During wants something times, it's not necessary to be rigid and unyielding but preferable to be calmly and firmly resolute to accomplish your goal.

Attention

Magda taught parents that it's far better to give a baby 100 percent attention *part* of the time rather than fractured attention *all* the time. In this day and age, when multitasking is the norm, it's important to remember that babies benefit from *undivided* attention, where the adult is completely tuned in to the baby and nothing else. This happens most often during caregiving routines and wants nothing times, which provide the baby with the opportunity to be emotionally refueled so that he can then contentedly be on his own, to rest or to enjoy uninterrupted play. Alternatively, when the adult's attention is always fractured or distracted, the baby's emotional needs are never completely satisfied, and he eventually learns that his parent's full attention is unattainable. In this case, he may simply and sadly give up.

Now that you've read about the RIE principles and key concepts, you may be wondering where to begin. I often suggest to new parents that they start by practicing just two things: slowing down and telling their babies what they're going to do before they do it. I ask them to notice how it feels for them and how their baby responds. The following chapters expand on the ideas and principles introduced in this chapter, and you will learn how to apply them in everyday situations with your baby.

2. At Home with Your Newborn

Dear new parent, do not be scared. Give in to the rhythm of a new biological clock; you will not stay in this place of time distortion forever.... Think of this as a kind of vacation on an island with no clocks, no duties other than responding to your own and your baby's rhythm and needs.

—Magda Gerber, *Dear Parent*

Unless you're a doctor or a nurse, caring for your newborn may be the first time that you've been so fully responsible for another person's life. Your newborn, of course, is not just any person. She is a precious child whose very life depends on you. Holding her in your arms for the first time, you may be flooded by powerful feelings of love and tenderness, and these may be coupled with anxiety, self-doubt, and despair. Your life has changed profoundly and dramatically.

The newborn period—the first twenty-eight days after birth—can be stressful for new parents as they try to understand what their baby needs. Getting to know your baby and understand her cues will take time, so try not to worry if you're at a loss in the first weeks. Eventually you'll begin to recognize the meaning of your baby's different cries, and you'll feel more confident. The more you pick up your baby and the more diapers you change, the more relaxed and confident you'll become. Understanding your baby and caring for her takes practice, so be kind to yourself as you find your way.

In the beginning, your baby will need your help to regulate her physical needs and her emotions. You'll notice she is tired, and lay her down in her crib so that she can rest. You'll feed her when you see that she's hungry. When she's upset, you'll speak soothingly to her to help her calm. Over time, she will begin to find ways to calm herself and manage her emotions in response to stress. She may suck on her fingers to self-soothe or turn away from a source of overstimulation. Learning to regulate her bodily functions and her emotions is a process that takes time, and she will need your sensitive, attentive, and responsive care to accomplish this. Having said this, it's important to know that even very sensitive parents miss many of their baby's cues. This is perfectly natural, but it is far easier to catch those cues when the adult is in a relaxed state rather than a hypervigilant one. Providing a peaceful environment and unhurried schedule, where your baby has the opportunity to turn her focus inward, can support her growing self-awareness and ability to self-regulate. It can also support your sense of calm.

TAKE CARE OF YOURSELF

After months, sometimes years, of anticipation, you are finally home with your newborn. Excited anticipation can turn to physical exhaustion, emotional anxiety, and even depression. Your schedule is topsy-turvy, and your sleep is continually interrupted. You may find yourself in a surreal haze as you try to understand your baby and take care of this new and important person in your life. To be able to take care of your baby, you need first to take care of yourself. If you're physically and emotionally depleted, you'll have little reserve remaining to care for your baby. Balancing your needs and your baby's can take some figuring out. So ask for and accept any offers of help. If a home-cooked meal makes you feel happy and well cared for, ask a few friends to deliver dinner for a week or three. If a yoga class helps keep you balanced, ask your partner or trusted friend to care for your baby so that you can make it to class. If a messy house puts you over the edge, then that's where you can ask for support in those first weeks home with your baby.

What about help that's offered when it's not asked for—unsolicited wisdom from well-meaning grandparents and friends with children of their own? Or worse still, criticism about how you're caring for your baby? It may be hard to speak your mind clearly when you're sleep deprived, but you may opt to gently remind the advice giver that although you appreciate their concern, *you* are the parent of this particular baby, and you need to practice to find your own way. The important thing is that *you* feel authentic about what you're doing, and that your interactions with your baby feel comfortable and right to you. Try to keep your focus on how *you* want to parent, and do your best to ignore what others are saying. As a parent recently told me, "My parents thought the 'RIE things' we were doing were strange and overly precious. I think they probably felt threatened because it's different from how they raised me. But now they see what a pleasure it is to be with their grandchild, who is cheerful and cooperative in ways they didn't think possible for a toddler. My mother recently acknowledged this and said she was glad I found RIE."

When you don't have the strength or the nerve to say no to a friend who wants to come "see the baby," ask your spouse or a friend to be the gatekeeper. Or before your baby is born, you might choose to establish a no visitors rule until your baby is one month old, inviting just a few people to visit initially if you like. As the parent of your newborn, it's up to you to advocate for her, sometimes with enthusiastic and excited friends and relatives who may want to hold or touch her. There may be times when it's appropriate for Grandma to hold her granddaughter, but when it's not, you might say, "I think she wants me to hold her now." You can send a clear message to the adult by speaking to your baby: "I think you might be getting hungry, so it's best if you stay in your bassinet until I feed you." This will sometimes be enough to slow people down and help make them aware that your baby is not a cute object to be held or played with for their enjoyment.

It was hard for me when people treated Briana like an object. I've probably done the same thing in the past, but I never understood it before I became a mother. She was just two weeks old, and people would say, "Let me touch her. Let me hold her," even when she was sleeping! Most people don't think babies have a point of view, so it wouldn't occur to them to look to the baby to see how she reacts to them as they try to touch or hold her.

— Rebecca Lovitz

THE ART OF OBSERVATION

Imagine that someone was caring for you and, without the benefit of conversation, had to figure out what you needed throughout the day and evening. Set aside the logic that your hunger usually arrives like clockwork—at 7:00, 12:00, and 7:00—and that you are always sleepy by 10:00. What if you were desperate for food but your caregiver guided you to your bed? How frustrating it would be if you wanted to rest but your caregiver offered you something to eat instead. Your true needs would remain unfulfilled, and you would be unable to fully relax and trust in your caregiver's ability to accurately care for you.

Observation is a key component of the Educaring Approach.

It will help you to slow down and learn to identify your baby's needs for food, rest, comfort, and engagement. It will help you get to know your baby better and discover what interests her. If your baby has been awake for a while and you think she may soon be sleepy, observe when her movements become less assured or when she lies very still. Does she rub her eyes or stare off dreamily? If your baby is sucking on her hand, this may be a sign that she is hungry. If she is looking at you and making a plaintive or demanding sound, perhaps she wants you to pick her up. You may learn to recognize other signs that are unique to your baby and are her way to indicate hunger, fatigue, or her need for emotional refueling.

Observation takes practice. You can begin by taking just five minutes to observe your baby while she is lying awake in her playpen. Find a comfortable place to sit near your baby where you can be quiet and still, and observe her as unobtrusively as possible. If you feel that your gaze is interrupting her, honor her sense of privacy by looking away from time to time. Practice observing with specificity. Here are just a few details you might look for: What attracts your baby's attention? Does she move her head in response to a sound or movement nearby? How are her arms and legs moving, and how long is she still before she moves again? What is your baby doing with her hands? Observe yourself. Are you able to remain focused and present with your baby, or does your mind wander? Is it easy or difficult to remain silent, or do you find yourself wanting to touch or talk to your baby? Did you notice anything for the first time, or did your baby surprise you in any way? As you become more and more comfortable observing your baby, you can increase the length of your observation. Many parents say they look forward to this time of quiet togetherness with their baby.

HOLDING YOUR BABY

Some parents ask, "How much should I hold my baby?" In the early weeks, you'll hold your baby a lot during feeding and at other times. What a pleasure it is to hold your baby and gaze at each other as she breast-feeds or has a bottle. Other than when she is being diapered or bathed, much of the time she'll be asleep. As her waking time increases, she will enjoy being held and cuddled by you, of course, but she will also benefit from having time to lie on her back in her crib, bassinet, or playpen. Parents are sometimes concerned that their baby may feel abandoned and unloved if they place her alone and awake in a crib. (While some babies may co-sleep with their parents or sleep in a crib or bassinet in the same room with their parents, I refer to baby sleeping in a crib in a separate room throughout the book.) They believe they need to hold her and give her their full attention whenever she is awake. Not only is this impossible for the parent, but it is also not ideal for the baby, who needs to be given the time and space to disengage from outside stimuli and turn her focus inward. Newborns and young babies like small, cozy spaces. In a crib, bassinet, or playpen, she will be free to stretch and move her limbs as she adapts to life outside the womb.

CRYING

A baby's cry can stir something deep within us. It may touch some unmet need lingering from our childhood or make us feel anxious that we haven't a clue what to do. How we respond to our baby's cry is, in part, determined by our particular temperaments and how we were cared for. When you cried as a child, how did your mother or father respond? Did someone offer a hug and ask what was the matter? Were you allowed to cry for as long as you needed, or was your upset minimized or even laughed at? Were you soothed with words and touch or told to toughen up and get on with it? If *you* had been the parent, is there anything you would have done differently?

When your baby cries, it may not be clear what she needs. If it takes some time for you to understand that she's not hungry but tired, she'll be fine. Every baby is unique, so give yourself time to get to know *your* baby. Do your best to relax, observe, and learn to understand what she's trying to tell you. You are embarking on a new relationship, after all, and relationships are not always straightforward and tidy. If you have the intention of wanting to understand your baby, that's a wonderful first step. As the weeks go by, you'll understand your baby's various cries more easily and begin to feel more confident in your responses and caregiving abilities. If you have a baby who cries a lot in the early weeks, do your best to take care of yourself and know that this phase will eventually end.

Crying is your baby's first language. She uses it to let you know when she is hungry, tired, or uncomfortable. Maybe she's too hot, too cold, or her Onesie is irritating her. She may cry when she's overstimulated, has gas, or startles from a loud sound. She may cry to release tension before falling off to sleep. It's not your task to stop the crying or to shorten its duration, but do try to understand *why* your baby is crying so that you can respond accurately. Don't assume that if your baby is crying, she needs you to comfort her. Some babies cry to self-soothe. Don't assume that if you're comforting your baby and she continues to cry, you must be doing something wrong or don't have the knack. Perhaps she's just not done crying yet. Babies do not cry to manipulate their parents; they cry to express a physical state or emotion. Therefore, responding to your baby's cry will not spoil her. In fact, responding accurately to your baby's needs will provide her with a sense of security, knowing that she's been heard and understood.

I was twenty-six when my son was born, and I had never been around babies before. I think I figured I had to do everything *at* them, like they were puppies or dolls. When I got pregnant, my parenting philosophy was "Love. Just love him so much and don't let him ever feel sad." Thank God I found RIE! RIE really allowed me to see Isaac as a person from the beginning — just an extra-small person. And unlike a doll, a person works things out, a person processes, a person cries — and it's all part of life. Now that he is four and a half, I truly feel that we have a relationship based on respect. I do my best to see him and hear him and, at the same time, stay true to my needs, and the rules and rhythms of our home.

— Frances Shaw

When your baby cries, it's not necessary to rush to her. Moving quickly may only increase her upset. Instead move slowly and let her know you're there. Speak calmly and soothingly to her. Refrain from saying, "You're okay." Instead you might say, "I hear you. I wonder why you're crying. You've just had a bottle, and you have a new diaper. Maybe you're telling me you're already sleepy and want to rest." Magda said that "allowing a child to cry requires more knowledge, time, and energy than just picking up a child and patting her."[1]

Don't distract your baby from her feelings by bouncing her on your knee or singing a cheery song. Trying to jolly your baby out of crying will only make her feel disconnected and out of tune with you. Imagine if you were upset and your trusted other responded with a big grin, spoke in a singsongy voice, and tried to humor you out of it. Think about how you would like someone to respond to you when you're upset.

All babies *need* to cry, for a variety of reasons. It's in the baby's best interest to be able to fully express how she feels. It's up to us to become comfortable with her crying. If you feel anxious when your baby cries, slow down and observe your baby. Observe yourself. Take a deep breath. Know that all emotions have a beginning and an end, so this crying, too, will eventually stop. It's far better to let emotions run their course than interrupt or thwart their expression. Talk to your baby. "You're crying very hard. I wish I knew what you needed right now, but I don't. Let's sit together and see if you can settle."

Many times over the years, a baby has cried inconsolably in an RIE Parent-Infant Guidance class, sometimes for quite a while. A mother may hold her baby and say, "I hear you crying. You can cry until you're all done." Just when it feels as if the baby's crying might go on forever, it suddenly stops, and the baby crawls down from her parent's lap, refreshed and renewed, ready to explore the play area. Crying can have a cleansing, relaxing effect and should be expressed freely.

Sometimes it may feel as if your baby has cried for an hour, but in fact, it has been only ten minutes. When your baby cries, think about her basic physical needs and ask these questions aloud: "Are you hungry? Do you need a new diaper?

Could you be tired already?" Just talking to your baby may help to release any anxiety you may feel. If the answer to all these questions is no, perhaps she is too warm or too cold or is not feeling well. Perhaps your baby is crying to express an emotional upset. Maybe she is startled or overstimulated. Rather than thinking about how to stop her crying, start by stating, in a soothing voice, what you observe. "You're really crying. I hear you." If she's lying down, you might touch her gently and then wait. Calming yourself can help you to stay present with your baby. If you feel tense, keep reminding yourself that it's natural for babies to cry, and trust that she will eventually stop. Just five minutes of constant crying can feel like an hour to parents. The more you're able to relax, the more likely you'll be able to refrain from bouncing, shushing, or pacing the hall to quiet her. These interventions may work in the moment, but babies quickly habituate to them, and before you know it, you may be rocking your crying baby for an hour in the middle of the night to soothe her. If you want to help your baby to calm, pay attention to your own breathing, your touch, your demeanor. Are you feeling tense, nervous, or angry? If so, your baby will likely pick up on your mood, and it may heighten her upset. You are an important mirror to your baby; your calmness can help her to calm, and vice versa. Understanding that babies need to cry, sometimes for what seems like a very long time, can help us to relax. Instead of feeling that you have to quiet the cry or "fix" something, practice giving your baby your attention and responding sensitively to her. Very often, just sitting and holding your baby quietly and letting her cry until she's all done will be all that she needs.

As I learned to take a moment before reacting to Liam's cry, I began to see and hear subtle differences in the quality of his cries. I heard the differences between the hungry cry and the tired cry. I started to see the faces and gestures he made when he was having a bowel movement. The other parenting literature I had read instilled in me this idea of what I *should* be doing or how Liam *should* be sleeping or eating. In RIE class, I learned to respond to my child as he was in that moment. I saw my son more clearly. He was asking for what he wanted, and I seldom felt as if I was guessing.

— Michael Cassidy

So often the breast or a bottle is offered as the cure-all when a baby cries or fusses. Parents can be in such a rush to silence the cry that they forget to first observe their baby to see what she actually needs so that they can respond accurately. This often happens because the cry makes parents anxious; their goal is to quiet the cry, which serves the parents' needs, but not necessarily the baby's. When we adjust the goal to first *understand* the cry, we respond to our babies more accurately.

It's helpful to remind yourself why your baby cries. Running through the following list of possibilities can help you to determine what your baby is trying to tell you when she's crying:

1. I'm hungry.
2. I'm tired.
3. I want my diaper changed.
4. I want to be picked up and held.

5. I'm too hot or too cold.
6. I'm overstimulated.
7. I don't feel well.

Pacifiers

Magda was opposed to pacifiers and wrote that popping a pacifier into a crying baby's mouth sends the message "I don't want to hear you. Stop crying." We've all seen a frustrated parent quickly thrust a pacifier into a sobbing baby's mouth, without even looking at, or speaking to, the baby. This is surely an example of what Magda was writing about. But *in the early weeks*, before your baby has the control to get her fist or fingers to her mouth, offering a pacifier to suck on may help your baby to soothe. Try to slow down and first observe your baby to determine whether or not she really needs a pacifier. Understand that if you offer it to her, she will very quickly come to expect the pacifier and will have a hard time doing without it. It's astonishing to see how quickly babies become conditioned to certain interventions; sometimes parents unintentionally create a need that wasn't really there to begin with. If you choose to offer a pacifier, it's very important that as soon as you see your baby push the pacifier out of her mouth when it's offered, you put it away. At that moment, let your baby's need to cry and desire to cry without the pacifier override your possible need for her crying to stop. When pacifiers are used insensitively and indiscriminately, they can harm the relationship between parent and baby because they send a message that the parent doesn't want to hear what the baby needs to express. Pacifiers also hinder a baby's ability to learn to self-calm. When a baby comes to rely on a pacifier instead of a thumb or finger or other means of self-soothing, it can be very difficult when that pacifier falls away from the nonmobile baby or out of the crib. Then, instead of relying on herself to soothe, the baby must rely on an adult to give her the soothing object. So if you choose to use a pacifier, do so judiciously. Offer it, observe closely to see if it helps your baby to calm, and put it away as soon as she shows you that she is no longer interested by pushing it out with her tongue or turning away from it.

When my son was an infant, around four weeks old, he had a pacifier with a small stuffed animal attached to the back. One day I heard him fussing and noticed that the pacifier had fallen out of his mouth. My initial reaction was to grab the pacifier and put it back in his mouth so that he would stop fussing, but he wasn't looking at me, and I had already recognized that when he really wanted help, he knew to look for a person, so I waited. To my amazement, he slowly worked the pacifier back up to his mouth with what ability he had — the tiny movements of his torso and head nudging the stuffed animal. I was reveling in this achievement when I watched him *spit out the pacifier* and start the whole process again! It was a game he was playing! If I had grabbed the pacifier and shoved it back into his mouth, I would have killed the game (and his motivation). After this, I tried to always wait for his signal that he needed me before stepping in. It was definitely difficult at times, especially when he was fussing and my mother was there! But I would just relate this story and explain why I was waiting.

— Arianne Groth

RHYTHM AND ROUTINE AND . . . SLEEP

The first days and weeks at home with your newborn can seem like a fog. It's hard to imagine that life goes on outside the cocoon you're living in with your baby. Trust that as you develop a rhythm and routine, the fog will lift, and you will begin to feel more yourself again. A large part of the adjustment to life with a newborn is learning to cope with interrupted sleep, so do your best to sleep when your baby sleeps. If you have a choice between returning a call and taking a nap, choose the nap. Take care of yourself by resting whenever you can. In the beginning, since your baby can't distinguish between night and day, you will have a twenty-four-hour schedule. Your baby may sleep more hours during the day than at night. In the early days, it may be all you can do to make sure that your baby's basic needs are met and yours are too, so try to let go of expectations and any desire to "get on a schedule." If you can feed and diaper your baby and also squeeze in a shower for you, great! When your baby is a few weeks older, more alert during the day, and sleeping more at night, you will settle into a more consistent rhythm, and routines will naturally develop.

Some babies have fairly predictable sleep schedules at a young age, and others seem to have little or no pattern at all for many months. It's important that sleep and feeding schedules follow the baby's cues rather than the baby following predetermined sleep and feeding schedules that may have little or no relation to her true rhythms and needs. You can certainly look to the clock to keep track of how much time has passed since your baby was last fed or rested, but then observe her to see if she's tired or hungry. Although your newborn will sleep much of the time, looking to her for signs of sleepiness is a good habit to get into right from the start. Likewise, you'll feed your baby when you observe that she's hungry rather than following a precise schedule. Of course, you might look at the time so that you can keep track of the last feeding (or use a handy smart phone app), then observe your baby to see if she's truly hungry, knowing that the ultimate answer will come from her.

What about Swaddling?

Just as she is about to get to sleep, you may be surprised to see your baby suddenly startle. Her arms and legs may twitch, or her whole body may shake and shudder. These involuntary movements are natural and will soon diminish. In the hospital, many newborn babies are immediately wrapped in tight swaddling blankets that bind the baby's arms and legs and restrict movement altogether. But Magda was opposed to anything that restricted free movement, and a tight swaddle certainly doesn't allow a baby to move her body. In a swaddling blanket, with her legs and arms tightly bound, a baby can't access her hands and fingers to self-soothe. Tight wrapping in the hip area can also increase the risk of developmental hip dysplasia.

I once took part in an RIE Foundations class exercise where I was swaddled as a way for me to experience things from a baby's point of view. Even before my partner had finished wrapping me, I panicked and instructed her to remove the swaddle as fast as she could. Ever since then, I've wondered if swaddled babies quiet down and go to sleep because it's preferable to feeling the panic or physical discomfort that comes with not being able to move.

A sleep sack, where your baby's arms and hands are free, can provide a much better alternative to a swaddling blanket. Since sleep sacks are loose around the hips and legs, your baby can rest on her back with her hips fully relaxed in an open position. A sleep sack should be used only in the first few months of your baby's life and should be dispensed with well before you observe your baby attempt to roll onto her side. By this time, she will need her arms, legs, and feet free to move so that she can use them to balance on her side.

COLIC

When a baby is irritable or crying for some unapparent reason, parents sometimes say that their baby is colicky or must be teething. Perhaps giving a label to things helps to soothe parents who dearly want to understand every cry and complaint emanating from their child. But colic is a confounding topic, and whether or not a baby is colicky can be subject to interpretation. Most babies are "fussy" toward the end of the day. They cry off and on, or continually, for a while. This is natural. These late afternoon and early evening periods of crying usually decline within a few months of age. But not all babies who cry inconsolably or for a long time are colicky.

A colicky baby cries persistently, at least three hours a day, at any time of the day or night, with little or no letup. In addition to crying, she may stiffen her limbs, extend her legs or pull them up to her stomach, arch her back, and howl with an intensity that may be alarming. A colicky baby is expressing physical discomfort. Colicky babies may have bloated, gassy stomachs that cause them a lot of pain. Some breast-feeding babies are sensitive to food in their mother's diet, and this may cause colic. Vegetables like broccoli and cabbage often produce a lot of gas, and citrus fruits, dairy, and other foods can be troublesome, too. If you think that something in your diet may be upsetting your baby's stomach, you may want to keep a log of what you eat and eliminate a few items at a time to see if your baby responds more positively. Colic can also be caused by an allergy to formula or gastroesophageal (acid) reflux. Both can cause abdominal pain and spitting up after feedings.

Some babies who are particularly sensitive to stimulation and more difficult to soothe are sometimes called colicky even though the discomfort is not physical. No matter the reason, long periods of crying can be physically and emotionally exhausting for new parents. At times like these, desperate parents resort to desperate measures like bouncing and rocking their babies, sometimes for hours on end. Instead do your best to create a peaceful and soothing environment for your baby: turn down the lights or turn them off completely; turn off the TV, radio, or music; pick up and carry your baby slowly; speak quietly; when you need to change her, move slowly and, as always, use gentle hands. Don't assume that your baby needs to be held all the time. It's possible that she'll be most comfortable lying on her back, where she can choose to extend her legs or pull them toward her tummy to help eliminate gas. If she has acid reflux, she'll need to spend some time upright.

If your baby is colicky, ask your doctor for medical advice, and enlist trusted friends and family to help by looking after your baby so that you can go for a walk or just get out of the house for a while.

*   *   *

In the newborn period, it may feel as if the days go by incredibly slowly, and then all of a sudden your baby is a month old! How has time moved so slowly, yet so quickly as well? Maybe it's the newness, joy, and wonder of it all, the intensity of emotion, the sleep deprivation. Be kind to yourself as you get to know your baby and find your way to establishing a rhythm and routine.

3. Caring for Your Baby

The way you care for your baby is how he experiences your love.

—Magda Gerber and Allison Johnson, *Your Self-Confident Baby*

Caregiving routines of diapering, bathing, and feeding are often thought of as "tasks" to hurry through so as to get on to something else. But a baby's day consists of caregiving routines, uninterrupted play, and sleep, so to what are we hurrying? And what message do we send to babies when we hurry through intimate caregiving moments in a brisk, mechanical way, without giving our full attention to the baby? Magda Gerber taught that caregiving times are relationship-building opportunities. When we believe that these times are important, we interact with our babies differently. We slow down. We give the baby our full attention. We ask for the baby's cooperation and participation. Caregiving is something we do *with* the baby, not *to* the baby.

RIE taught me that every custodial task (changing a diaper or providing food) is an opportunity to connect with your child. It completely changed my perspective from the obligation of performing a task for someone else (servitude) to the opportunity to share a meaningful moment with someone I love.

— Chet Callahan

A baby's sense of trust begins in his body. Does he feel secure when he is picked up, laid down, and carried? Can he relax in the arms that hold him, or does he tense up, unable to fully relax? Are the hands that touch him gentle and confident or rough, insecure, indifferent? When he looks into his caregiver's eyes, does he feel connected, seen, and understood, or do the eyes seem vacant and distant? The way we care for our babies, the touch of our hand, the tone of our voice and our gestures—these together express how we feel about them, how we value and love them. A baby's sense of self and self-worth is reflected back to him in these shared, intimate caregiving moments.

The person who believes a baby is utterly helpless will care for a baby in a very different way from one who believes that a baby has thoughts, feelings, and a unique point of view and level of competence. When we believe that a baby can participate, our behavior changes. When we communicate to the baby about what we're doing together, we invite the baby to take part. We send the message that the baby's participation is valued and important to us. When the baby participates, his competence is revealed to us. It can be surprising to see just how capable even a young baby can be. During a diaper change, we might say, "Would you lift your bottom for me?" At first, inviting a baby to participate may feel awkward and strange. But when you involve your baby, you are saying, "I value your participation. You're competent. We can do this together." New parents and other caregivers are often surprised by how much a baby can actually understand and do. Inviting participation helps to build cooperation, develop focus and attention, and create a deeper connection between parent and baby.

DAY IN, DAY OUT CAREGIVING

What's your morning routine? Do you jump out of bed when the alarm goes off, flick on the coffee machine, head to the bathroom to shower, do your hair and dress in a particular sequence, gulp down a cup of coffee, and charge out the door? Or do you hit the snooze button three times before getting up, lay out your clothes before heading to the bathroom, eat a leisurely breakfast while reading the newspaper, and then start your day? Whatever your routine, it probably varies little from day to day. If one little thing goes awry, you can feel off balance, and the day can get off to a bumpy start. If several things in your routine don't go as they usually do, you may think, "What's going on here?" Most of us prefer consistency, routine, and regularity when it comes to our everyday care.

So does your baby.

An important aspect of any caregiving task is having a predictable routine. This helps the baby to feel secure because he learns to anticipate what will happen next and can participate when he is able. Having a predictable rather than a do-what-you-will approach lets the baby know what your expectations are and sets the stage for discipline. No matter what the task, here are some basic caregiving concepts.

- **Prepare the environment ahead of time.** Once you bring your baby to the changing table, bath, or feeding area, you should be fully involved with whatever you're doing together, without interruption. Prepare the bottle ahead of time, not with your baby in your arms. Lay out everything you need for the bath and fill the tub with water before carrying your baby to the bathroom. Check to see that you have diapers, wipes, and a fresh Onesie before carrying your baby to the changing table.

- **Go slowly.** Help your baby focus on the task at hand by slowing down, waiting, and giving him the opportunity to prepare for what will happen next. Allow time for him to make eye contact with you, follow your actions, vocalize, and otherwise respond to you—and you to him. Going slowly helps to create a sense of calm. A diaper change that happens in a quick flurry of activity doesn't give your baby the opportunity to follow each step in the process. When you slow down, your baby can observe and eventually learn each step of the predictable routine. As the routine becomes familiar, he can anticipate what will happen next, making it possible for him to participate cooperatively when he is able. It may be hard to imagine, but your young baby will eventually bathe and dress himself. If you slow down so that he is able to participate in his care from the very beginning, he will gradually take on more and more of his self-care, with competence and confidence.

- **Narrate.** It's certainly not necessary or even advisable to give a running commentary during caregiving routines. If there is constant chatter, just as an adult would, your baby may opt to tune out. Tell your baby what's going to happen next. "I know that you're hungry. I'm going to the kitchen to make your bottle." "It's time to wash your hair. I want to wet your hair first. Can you lean your head back for me?" If you narrate each step along the way, your baby can relax, knowing that he'll always be told what's going to happen next, and there will be no surprises.

Narrating is an important part of creating a sense of trust with your baby. It can also help you to stay present with your baby rather than having your mind wander to the phone call you have to make or the work you need to finish later today. It's sometimes difficult to remain focused and present with someone who can't respond to you verbally, so talking about what you're doing together can help you to stay attuned to your baby.

Caregiving is a back-and-forth dance between you and your baby. Narrate what you're doing together and ask your baby for his cooperation. Look into his eyes when you speak to him and respond to his gestures and vocalizations. One way that babies acquire language is by being spoken to, of course, so it makes sense to speak to him about what you're doing together. Even though your baby or toddler may not yet be speaking in recognizable words, he's conveying a lot through his eyes, facial expression, and gestures. If your baby points at something, incorporate that into your conversation.

In the beginning, your baby may only look in your eyes as you speak to him. But as you get in the habit of narrating, your baby will learn to understand what you're saying and will participate when he is able and interested in doing so. When you say, "It's time to take off your diaper," you will be delighted when one day he squeals and lifts his legs. When you tell him it is bath time, he may coo and kick with excited anticipation. By observing your baby, narrating, and responding to his sounds and gestures, you are laying the foundation for a lifetime of respectful, reciprocal communication between you.

- **Allow tarry time.** When you're diapering, bathing, or feeding your baby, give tarry time so that he can process what you've told him and what's happening before moving on to the next step. Rather than scooping up your baby without warning, greet him, tell him what you'd like to do, and wait—give him time to take in what you've said and ready himself. "Alex, I see you're playing with the cup, but I'd like to pick you up so that we can change your diaper." Wait until he's processed what you've said and shows that he's ready. Perhaps he listened to you and then turned his attention back to the cup. Then you might say, "Alex, it looks like you're not quite ready. We can wait a minute." Then... wait a minute. If the time passes and he's still not ready, you can say, "Alex, it looks like you're still enjoying the cup, but it's time to change your diaper now." Wait a few moments to give your baby time to take in what you've said, and tell him that you're going to pick him up. Move slowly. He may protest and reach for the cup. If he does, you might say, "You're reaching for the cup. I know you want to keep playing, but it's time to change your diaper now. You can play with the cup when we're done." While it might seem easier to let your baby play with an object during a diaper change, it distracts his attention from you and what is happening to his body, and the diaper change devolves from something intimate you are doing *together* to something you are doing to or for your baby.

- **Establish predictability and routine.** Your baby won't be bored by following the same simple routine each time; he will actually enjoy it. Over time, he'll come to understand, anticipate, and participate more and more in his care. Do your best to diaper, bathe, and feed your baby in the same place each time. There are times when changes to routine must happen, whether it's as simple as a houseguest or as complex as moving to a new home. At these times, the routines of daily life take on even more importance, as they provide the child with something that is reliably consistent.

- **Give your full attention.** Turn off the phone and ask others not to interrupt when you're about to diaper, bathe, or feed your baby. Whenever possible, anticipate and ignore interruptions. Let phone calls go to voice mail. Treat caregiving time as special one-to-one time. When you give your undivided attention to your baby, the message you send is "I care about you. This time is just for us." Of course, interruptions do sometimes happen. An older child may ask for something, or some other unanticipated interruption may occur. When this happens, do your best to make the disruption as brief as possible and apologize to your baby for the interruption—just as you would to an adult.

PICKING UP YOUR BABY

What's the first step before diapering, bathing, or feeding your baby? You must first pick him up! Most adults carry even their very young babies upright against their chest, with the baby's head facing their shoulder. But Dr. Pikler and Magda Gerber taught that babies should never be put into a position they can't get into on their own. This means that before a baby is able to sit up on his own, he should be carried in the horizontal position, with his head, neck, and spine fully supported. Here's how:

Move slowly, go to your baby's level, and speak softly to let him know you're there. Make eye contact. If he's on his back, gently touch his chest; if he's on his tummy, gently touch his back. Tell him that you'd like to pick him up. Pause and give tarry time to let him take in what you've said. Look for a cue that he's ready to be picked up. You may feel his chest or his back relax, he may begin to squirm in anticipation of being picked up, or he may hold his arms out to you.

You can pick your baby up no matter what direction he's facing, but here we'll assume he's on his back, with his head to your left side. First, lift his right shoulder slightly with your right hand so that you can slide your left hand and forearm under his head and down so that they're supporting his spine and his bottom. Slide your right hand and forearm under his legs and bottom so that he is resting comfortably in your arms, with his head resting in the crook of your left arm. Check to see that his head, neck, and spine are fully supported. Be sure that his arm has not gotten stuck under your arm; both arms and legs should be in front of your baby so that he can move them freely. From this "cradle" position, your baby will be in a position to be able to gaze up at you, his "secure base."

If he's on his tummy, support his head, gently roll him over onto his back, and pick him up as noted earlier.

To lay your baby down, lower his bottom onto the blanket, crib, or other surface first, then slowly lower the rest of his body. As his chest lowers, slide out the arm that was below his legs and take his head in that hand. Then slide out the other hand, cradle his head in both hands, and slowly lower it. Try to do this as smoothly and slowly as possible.

When your baby is able to get to the sitting position on his own, then carrying him in an upright position can be familiar and comfortable for him.

BATHING

Bath time can be pleasurable for both of you, as your baby enjoys being held in the water, moves his arms and legs about, and splashes playfully. Newborns, who can be sensitive to changes in temperature, may not enjoy the bath at first, so you may choose to sponge bathe your newborn during the first weeks of life. It may be preferable to soap and shampoo your young baby and only bring him to the tub to rinse, thus avoiding a long time in the water. You can do this on a mat next to the tub or on the changing table. Cover either area with a waterproof cloth or cover with a towel on top. Lay your baby down on top of the towel, and as you wash him, use it to cover the rest of his body so that he doesn't get cold. As always, observe your baby to see how he responds. When you place him in the water, hold him gently but securely. It's not necessary to fill the tub with water; just a few inches will do.

- **Prepare ahead.** Gather everything you will need — washcloth, soap, shampoo, towel, and a few bath toys (for toddlers) — so that it is close at hand and ready to use. Prepare the bathwater ahead of time before bringing your baby to it.

- **Go slowly.** When you move slowly to put soap on the washcloth or shampoo in your hand, your baby can follow along with what you're doing, participate when he's able, and relax and enjoy the bath. Observe to see that you're moving slowly enough that he can be in rhythm with you.

- **Narrate.** What is there to talk about during the bath? Here's just an example of the kind of language you might use: "I'm putting soap on the washcloth. Can you turn your head this way? I'd like to wash behind your ears. Now I'll wash your forehead and your cheeks. Would you lift your chin so I can wash your neck?" It's not necessary to recite a monologue, but do communicate with your baby about what's happening next and respond to what interests him.

- **Allow tarry time.** After you tell your baby what's about to happen, give him time to take in what you've said, and observe when he's ready for the next step. In this way, he can feel secure, knowing there will be no unexpected surprises, and can participate when he's ready.

- **Establish predictability and routine.** You can do this in a variety of ways, one of which is to bathe your baby in the same head-to-toe sequence each time. In this way, he'll learn that the bath is complete after his feet have been washed. If he's old enough to play with bath toys, he'll know that the play objects can come into the tub after this final step has been completed.

Rather than the bath being a haphazard whirlwind of soap and shampoo, following a predictable sequence allows the child to understand each step of the process and, when he's ready, begin to take on more of the bathing routine himself.

A sixteen-month-old child has a runny nose, and you want to wipe it. You have learned that it is important to approach her from the front so that she can see you, to respect her by telling her what you plan to do and asking for her cooperation. But you have learned from this child that the quickest and cleanest way to wipe her constantly running nose is to catch her unaware from behind, hold her head, wipe, and walk away before she has time to flee from you and press her face into the couch. What to do?

Moments like these are key moments for carers. How do you move Educaring ideas into practice in the moment, and why should you?

First, this child has learned she can trust you to care for her. She is learning about her place in the world. Is she a person who participates? Is she included in decisions about her day, or is she a person who has things done to her? You ask her to respect your body and the bodies of her friends. She is not supposed to push, poke, or pull on other children. She is learning this lesson. But is she given a consistent message? Is she offered the same respect? Each time her nose is wiped before she knows what is happening, each time she is picked up from behind in the middle of play for a diaper change, each time her carer laughingly tells a story about her to another adult and she hears it, she is given a message, and that message is "be passive, give in, and accept," her body is not her own, her concentration on a task is not recognized or valued, her contribution to tasks is not important.

When you see her, do you see a child who has had all the experiences that a toddler's morning brings, who is interested in things with wheels and loves toast, and whose favorite part of the day is cuddling with you to read books? Or do you see a nose with mucus coming out?

Let her know that you see her nose is running and needs to be wiped. Bring the tissue box and let her pull one out and take the first pass at her nose. Then ask for the tissue and tell her you would like to finish the job. If possible, provide a mirror so that she can watch the process. Engage her in hand washing, too. Give her a chance to be an initiator and a participant in the process. You may even go so far as to make it a special moment between you, a chance for her to have an extra squeeze if she wants it.

Even though you make these changes, she might still try to run to the couch and wipe her nose on it. After you approach her with the tissue box and she starts to bolt, kneel and catch her. You can stop her by holding her body in your arms and making eye contact. You can explain that you need to wipe her nose before she runs to the couch. Give her a moment to cooperate and then gently wipe her nose. Over time, if you are consistent, she will participate and cooperate. She may even ask you to help her sometimes. At some point, you may be able to leave tissues out on a table or shelf near the mirror.

— Deborah Greenwald, RIE Associate

DIAPERING

Diapering is traditionally thought of as a hygienic task to prevent diaper rash and keep a baby clean, dry, and comfortable. But Magda taught us that it can be so much more. It's an opportunity for your baby to emotionally refuel and for relationship building. When we consider that most babies will be diapered more than five thousand times in their young lives, diaper changing takes on considerably more significance. Why not make the most of these moments together? New parents often say, "Between diapering, feeding, and attending to my baby's needs—not to mention my own—I have no time or energy left just to be with my baby." But changing your baby's diaper *is* "being" with him, so whenever you can, take your time and enjoy accomplishing this task together.

The adult's approach to diapering can make all the difference. When diapering is seen as a chore, a messy task to be completed as quickly as possible, the adult may do it briskly and efficiently, perhaps putting a toy in the baby's hand to distract him. There is little eye contact or communication as the adult concentrates on the lower half of the baby's body. If the baby cries or protests, the adult may speed up the pace, telling the baby, "We will be through in no time, and then you can play."

But what does this tell the baby? A brisk, mechanical style of diapering sends a negative message—that caring for the body and for bodily functions is unpleasant. This idea is reinforced when a toy is given to distract the baby while he's being diapered. He learns to tune out rather than feel the indifferent way in which his body is being handled and the emotional disconnect with the adult. He gets in the habit of turning his attention away from his body, away from the task in progress, and away from his parent or caregiver.

On the other hand, when we see diapering as an opportunity for intimacy and learning, it takes on profound significance and meaning. When done sensitively, diapering can provide your baby with a sense of security, a feeling of being respected and tenderly cared for. He can sense how you feel through your hands, your voice, and your gaze.

Prepare what you need ahead of time. Have everything—diapers, fresh clothes, wipes, creams—ready before you bring your baby to the changing table. Turn off the phone so that you won't be interrupted. Tell your baby, "I'm turning off the phone now because this time is just for you and me." Saying this aloud reinforces how important this time together is for both of you.

Move slowly, approach your baby, and tell him that you'd like to change his diaper. If he's distracted on the changing table, wait for his attention before you begin.

Narrate what's going to happen next and invite him to participate. Remember to give **tarry time** so that he can process what you're telling him. If he doesn't participate, know that he will soon understand the meaning of what you're saying. Cooperation is a possibility but certainly doesn't always happen.

A diapering narration might go something like this but should not be a running commentary (there will also be times, when your baby is tired or in the middle of the night, when few or no words will be necessary): "Nate, I want to take off your leggings. Will you lift your bottom so I can pull them down? [Baby lifts bottom; adult removes leggings.] Now let's take off your diaper. Do you want to open the tabs? [Remember, babies are competent!] It looks like you don't want to do that right now, so I will. [Open Velcro tab.] It makes a sound. Now I'll open the other tab. [Pick up soiled diaper, show to baby.] Here's your soiled diaper. I'm going to fold it up and put it in the bin. [Gently touch behind baby's knees.] Can you lift your bottom for me? [If baby doesn't lift bottom, put hands or forearm behind baby's knees and lift up. Don't hold ankles together and lift from there, as this causes reflexive arching of the back that tightens the bottom, making it difficult to wash properly; it's also uncomfortable for baby.] Now I'm going to wipe your bottom. [Show baby the wipe.] The wipe's a little cold. Here's your new diaper. [Show baby new diaper.] I want to slide it under your bottom. Thank you. Now you can put your legs down. [Lift diaper up over baby's tummy and fold in sides.] Would you like to press the tabs? [Baby doesn't respond, so mother closes tabs.] [Baby looks at light and then at mother.] You were looking up at the light. [Pause and wait for baby's attention.] Let's put your leggings back on. [Touching one leg.] Can you lift this leg for me? [Pull legging over one leg.] How about the other leg? Let's pull these up over your bottom. All done. [Pause.] [Mother gestures with palms up in front of her.] Are you ready for me to pick you up? [Picks up baby. If it's still time to play, to maintain a sense of continuity, lay baby back down next to the object he was playing with.] I'm going to lay you back down. There's your ball. I'm going to wash my hands, and I'll be right back."

Once your baby becomes more mobile, diapering may become more of a challenge, because chances are good he won't want to lie still on the changing table. He may roll over onto his tummy or push up onto all fours. What's to be done? First of all, it can be helpful to let go of your expectations. Your baby isn't moving because he is being contrary; he just loves to be in motion. So it's unrealistic to expect him to happily lie still for a diaper change.

Practice accommodating your moving baby by learning to wash his bottom and put on a new diaper while he's on all fours. If your baby is standing, he can stand on the floor, holding on to a firm surface, while you change his diaper. This may sound crazy, but adapting your style of diapering to accommodate a moving baby can prevent diaper changes from becoming a battleground. It can take practice to diaper a baby who is not flat on his back, but it can be done.

When trying to diaper a baby who is wiggly and uncooperative, the tendency is to speed things up to get the diaper changed as quickly as possible. But what happens when we move quickly? Our touch becomes less gentle, and we lose our connection with the baby. We become frustrated, and the baby becomes agitated. So slow down; maybe even stop for a moment. Look at your baby and speak to him, acknowledging his point of view. "I know it's hard to lie still when you want to move. But we need to change your diaper. Can you lie still for me for just a minute longer? I want to take off your soiled diaper and wash your bottom." He may still wiggle, and you may have to gently but firmly keep him from moving so that you can accomplish the task. Pay attention to your tone of voice and your breathing. If you're feeling frustrated, tell your baby. "I'm frustrated. When you wiggle, it makes it hard to change your diaper." Sometimes, just by saying the words aloud, our frustration dissipates.

DRESSING YOUR BABY

Imagine you are unable to dress yourself. How you would like to be touched and moved? You would probably prefer to be moved slowly and gently, and as little as possible. It would be difficult to relax if you were turned brusquely from side to side or had your head lifted up more than just slightly. When dressing or undressing your baby, try to move the garment to accomplish the task rather than moving your baby. In other words, do your best to move your baby's limbs as little and as gently as possible, and move the garment to pull it on or off your baby. When putting on a sweater, for instance, put your hand through the sweater from the shoulder to the wrist, so that your fingers are poking out of the wrist end of the sleeve. Now place the bunched-up sleeve over your baby's hand and, while gently holding his hand, pull it up your baby's arm and over his shoulder. Do the same on the other side. When putting a Onesie on your baby, gather it up, lift your baby's head as little as possible from the changing table, and pull the neck opening of the Onesie over your baby's head. Next gather up each sleeve and put it on as described in the sweater example. Last, gently lift your baby's bottom from the changing table and pull the Onesie down over his chest and bottom.

FEEDING

Whether your baby is breast-feeding, drinking from a bottle, or eating at a table, it's important to have reasonable expectations and to provide an appropriate environment, one that is predictable and as peaceful as possible. In this way, the child can focus on his inner rhythms of hunger and satiation while getting nourishment and paying attention to his body's cues. He'll eat when he's hungry and stop when he's satisfied. For him to accomplish this successfully, it's important to minimize other input that might distract him from the feeding experience. This means that you might have to forgo the "family meal" for a couple of years to provide a focused mealtime for your baby. If you have read how important it is for a family to eat their meals together, this advice may seem confusing, but sitting at the table, sharing a meal together with the whole family, is something that will happen more successfully when your child is a bit older. It is unreasonable to expect a baby or young toddler to sit at the table while you're trying to have a civilized, leisurely meal, and most parents enjoy their meals a lot more when they are not also tending to their baby or young toddler. In a short time, your toddler will be older and will have mastered self-feeding, at which time it will be a pleasure to eat together at the dinner table and have a delightful conversation with your child. In the meantime, try not to hurry things, and do your best not to have unreasonable expectations that your baby or young toddler can't yet fulfill. Turn off the phone and TV, shut down the computer, and enjoy being fully present with your baby during feeding times.

To help a baby learn to eat when he's hungry and stop eating when he's satiated, we need to observe closely so that we're attuned to his cues. Then we need to honor what the baby communicates to us. You may be able to discern your baby's "hungry cry," or you may notice that he smacks his lips or "roots" when he wants to be fed. Wait for him to calm before offering the bottle or breast. When is your baby done eating? When he says so or indicates that he is done by pulling off the bottle or breast, pursing his lips, or turning away from the food. Babies should never be coaxed, cajoled, or forced to eat. They should eat however much they want, and not one bite more! If you're concerned that your baby hasn't eaten a lot but is clearly saying, "I'm done," respect what he's telling you. If you're worried that he isn't getting enough nourishment, keep a journal for a week and write down how much your baby is eating (or how long he's nursing and how vigorously), and at what time each day. You may be surprised by just how much your baby *has* consumed. Remember that babies' stomachs are very small, the size of a marble at birth, a Ping-Pong ball at ten days. Sometimes babies eat a lot one day and very little the next. They may eat more than usual just before a growth spurt and very little when they're not feeling well. Just as most of us don't eat a consistent amount every single day, babies don't either. And just as we would never tell an adult how much to eat, practice giving the same respect to your baby. When you do, you'll be supporting him to self-regulate, and mealtime will be a pleasure for both of you.

Your pediatrician will likely help you determine when to begin feeding your baby solid foods, most often sometime around six months. Your baby will not only become accustomed to new tastes and smells, but also learn how to take food from a spoon. Rather than introducing new tastes *and* spoon-feeding simultaneously, begin by offering breast milk or formula from a spoon to start. Do this a few times a day until your baby becomes familiar and comfortable taking breast milk or formula from the spoon. You can follow these "spoon experiences" by offering the breast or bottle to be sure his hunger is satisfied. In a short time, he will become familiar with the spoon, and you can offer him first food from the spoon. When introducing new foods, offer the same food for three to four days to see how your baby responds. By doing this, you will immediately know the cause if he has an allergic reaction, such as a rash, vomiting, or diarrhea.

Where should you feed your baby? Feed him in the same quiet place each time. What about a high chair? From your baby's point of view, imagine eating entirely new foods from a strange utensil in the comfort of your parent's warm and familiar lap versus being suspended high off the ground in a high chair or being strapped into a bouncy seat. Many babies who are placed in high chairs are not yet able to sit up unassisted. Since they are not able to hold themselves upright, they may slide farther and farther down in the high chair. This certainly can't be comfortable for the baby, nor is it an ideal position for breathing comfortably and taking in food. The high chair also takes away the toddler's ability to move away from the table when he's done eating. Instead he has to rely on the adult to release him from captivity.

Magda taught that all feeding should be done on the parent's lap until the baby is able to sit up by himself and support his upper trunk. Being held by you as he tries new foods for the first time and learns to eat from a spoon will provide your baby with physical security and emotional support. Once he is able to sit up on his own, your baby can eat from a folding tray table placed on the floor. When a toddler is walking securely, he can progress to eating at a toddler-size table while sitting on a toddler-size stool. Stools are preferable to a chair because the child can climb on from any side of the stool, and it is less complex to navigate than a chair. It's important that the stool is short enough that the toddler's feet are able to be flat on the floor. In this position, he is able to sit securely and focus on eating. Refrain from putting your child on the stool but rather let him find his way himself. It may take a few days or weeks for your child to figure out how to get onto the stool, but in time he will be able to do so with ease and confidence. The progression from lap feeding to tray table to toddler-size table is informed not only by your child's gross motor readiness but also by his psychological readiness. Some babies will prefer to sit on their parent's lap to eat long after they are able to sit up on their own; others will prefer to sit on the floor at a tray table even though they are able to sit on a stool.

It's important not to push your child before he is ready but instead to allow his readiness to unfold over time. RIE friend and mentor Carol Pinto wrote about a child with special needs named Molly and described how her caregiver was sensitively attuned to her cues. Molly's parents had engaged the services of an early interventionist to help her develop motor skills. Most of the time, Molly drank from a bottle, but sometimes she enjoyed drinking from a cup. One day, Molly's "interest in drinking stopped abruptly. The caregiver, respecting her desires, did not try to entice her. When the therapist next appeared at the center she remarked that she and Molly had been 'working' on using the cup. Molly's caregiver believed that Molly's refusal to continue using the cup was based on this pressure, however subtle and well-intended, to achieve a behavioral objective. Perhaps, Molly's resistance to an externally imposed objective might even be seen as a sign of self-respect."[1]

Breast or Bottle Feeding

Identify a place that will be comfortable for you and your baby so that you can both relax and enjoy this time together. For a young baby, feed him in the same place—same chair, same room—whenever possible. Remember that feeding is a time to be completely present with your baby, so turn off the TV, music, and cell phone so that you can both focus on the feeding.

Sometimes I make fun of Rebecca when she's nursing the baby. She just sits back and says, "Can you get me the water?" I'm going to make a tool belt so that she can put everything she needs there! I compare it to when I'm in the kitchen cooking. I always visualize what I need beforehand — the ingredients and the utensils — so I have everything organized. Then I start cooking. When Rebecca has the baby and starts nursing her, she always needs a tissue, or her water is in the other room. Sometimes she calls me from the cell phone because she doesn't want to yell.

— Alfonso Ortega

- **Prepare ahead.** Have a bib, a warmed bottle if using pumped milk or formula, and a burping cloth at the ready before you sit down with your baby to offer him the breast or bottle. For nursing moms who need to stay hydrated, it's good to have a glass of water within reach.

- **Go slowly.** If your baby is crying loudly because he's hungry, do your best to move slowly as you prepare his bottle or get settled in your chair to nurse him. Moving slowly conveys a sense of calm and can help your baby to calm, even when he's very hungry. When you are prepared and have your baby in your arms, look to see if he's ready. Is he opening his mouth? Rooting for the breast? If he's grunting impatiently, pause for a moment and let him calm. *Offer* the breast or bottle rather than placing the nipple in your baby's mouth. Let your baby choose when to latch on and suck.

- **Narrate.** Talk about what you're doing together when there's really something to say, but do so without unnecessary chatter. "You're ready for your bottle. There you go." "Mmm. You were very hungry." When your baby shows you that he's had enough, you might say, "You've pushed the nipple out of your mouth. You must be done."

- **Allow tarry time.** Your baby may be hungry, but is he ready to take the breast or bottle in his mouth? Pause and wait for a cue that he's ready.

  When it's time for burping, lift the arm that's supporting your baby's head so that he's in a slightly more upright position...and then wait. This is all you need to do. Placing him against your shoulder and striking him on the back does little to extract a burp and is really rather violent.

- **Establish predictability and routine.** Feeding your baby in the same place each time, without something new and unfamiliar to distract him, lets him focus on feeding and enjoy being with you. He receives nourishment and emotional refueling from this togetherness.

Night Feedings

Because their digestive systems are small, newborns need to be fed in the middle of the night, but how do you get your baby to taper off when the feedings have become a habit rather than a physiological necessity? Some parents say, "My ten-month-old baby is still waking up at 2:00 a.m. for a feeding. How can I get him to let go of those feedings so I can get a decent night's sleep?"

When you first hear your baby cry, don't immediately roll out of bed, rush to his crib or into his room, turn on a light, and pick him up. That would certainly rouse him. Wait, and then wait a little more. Listen to his cry. If he's not a newborn or young baby who needs to be fed often, see if you can understand what his cry is telling you. It may be that he doesn't actually need you but will settle back down to sleep. If the breast or bottle is offered and your baby sucks vigorously, it will be clear that your baby is hungry and needs to be fed. In this case, make your visit as boring as you can and all about feeding so that you don't stimulate him. If possible, don't brighten the light in the room. There may be no need to talk, and unless he has pooped or has a leaky diaper, a change is not necessary. In the middle of the night, you will naturally want to expedite things to get back into your cozy bed, but try to slow yourself down so that you can listen and observe what your baby really needs.

Weaning

At some point, your baby may show less interest in breast-feeding. Some mothers, who may be enjoying the intimacy that breast-feeding provides, may miss their baby's cues of waning interest or may unconsciously ignore them to prolong this special sense of closeness. Their baby may be ready for breast-feeding to come to an end before they are. But as one chapter of the parenting journey ends, so another begins. There is much joy to be had in following your baby's lead as he lets you know that he's ready for what comes next. Learning to observe and let go of our own agendas to support our child's readiness is an important and valuable parenting lesson. There are also times when a mother wants to wean her baby before he is ready. This can occur when a mother feels burdened by breast-feeding—because she is physically tired, "wants her body back," or because she has to go back to work and feels that pumping her breast milk will be a challenge in the work environment. She may feel pressure from friends or relatives who subtly or openly assert that it's time for her baby to be weaned. Since weaning involves setting limits as you begin to eliminate one feeding and then another, it is important for you to clearly convey your intention to your child. If you feel guilty, doubtful, or otherwise ambivalent, your child will pick up on this, and the weaning process will likely be more challenging.

Whatever the case, weaning can take several weeks or months and can happen either relatively smoothly or with some difficulty. Rather than abruptly stopping breast-feeding altogether, eliminate feedings gradually, letting go of one feeding at a time, beginning with the one your baby seems the least interested in. The morning and evening feedings are usually the most precious, and the feeding right before bedtime is the one that children are likely to have the hardest time letting go of. For this reason, don't make the before-bedtime nursing the last one you eliminate. Many mothers start by eliminating the postnap nursing, eventually let go of the morning nursing, and end with eliminating the evening feeding. If your child asks to nurse at a feeding time you've eliminated, you can tell him, "We're not going to nurse now. If you're thirsty, you can have some water." If your child protests or becomes upset, hold firm and offer an alternative. "It's not time to nurse, but I'll be happy to sit and cuddle with you." Let weaning happen gradually, with love and compassion.

Lap Feeding

You may want to wear an old shirt or smock over your clothes, or something that you won't mind getting messy. On a table next to where you'll be sitting with your baby, place a bib, a damp washcloth, a small, clear glass containing food, a serving bowl with extra food, one serving and two feeding spoons, a short water glass (that your baby can get his hands around), and a one- or two-cup pitcher of water. Think about the feeding equipment you're using and choose items that will be the easiest for your baby to practice with as he masters his self-feeding skills. I recommend that parents use a small, clear glass for drinking. These allow your baby to see what is in the glass, and help to create good habits of holding the glass properly so that the liquid won't spill. Shot glasses can be good to start with because they are easy to grasp. At RIE, we use small Duralex Picardie glasses because they are durable.

■ Cradle your baby on your lap so that he's sitting sideways, with your arm behind his back, and his neck and head supported by your shoulder and upper arm. His arms and legs are in front of him, free to move. You've washed his hands with the washcloth and put on his bib. If you're holding him in your left arm, hold the glass containing the food in your left hand. With your other hand, take some food onto the spoon. Hold the spoon out in front of your baby, just above his eye level, and show him the food. "I have some cereal for you." Let him have control over his feeding by waiting for him to give you a cue that he's ready before bringing the spoon to his lips. He may open his mouth or make a sound of excited anticipation. (For a baby just starting to use a spoon, touching the spoon to his bottom lip will cause him to open his mouth.) Gently slip the spoon into his mouth, tip the handle up slightly so that the top lip "cleans" food off the spoon when it's removed from his mouth, and take care not to touch the spoon to the roof of his mouth.

▪ Feeding is about reciprocity, so wait until your baby signals that he would like more before offering another spoonful. He may open his mouth or make a sound to indicate that he wants more. Avoid shoveling food into your baby's mouth.

▪ If your baby wants to take the spoon and feed himself, let him do so. Support his exploration and desire for autonomy by letting him hold the spoon. You can then put food onto the second feeding spoon and have a sort of (slow-moving) assembly line where you fill the spoon with food and offer it to him to bring to his mouth. Remember that no child can master self-feeding without creating at least a little bit of a mess. A spoon that is intended for the mouth may arrive somewhere closer to his ear on the first several tries. If you're someone who likes things to be neat and tidy, this may be a challenge for you. Try to appreciate your baby's curiosity and desire and practice letting go of your need for tidiness.

▪ Your baby may grab the spoon on its way to his mouth. He may enjoy the sensation of squishing the yogurt through his fist and then sucking it off his fingers. Touching the yogurt may provide a sensory experience that the spoon cannot, or he may not be comfortable with the spoon just yet. As long as he is actively engaged in eating, and as long as you can tolerate some messiness, it's okay to give your baby the latitude to explore the food in this way.

▪ If you run out of food in the glass that you're holding and your baby is still hungry, refill it from the serving bowl that you've set nearby.

▪ Observe your baby for cues that his hunger has been satisfied: he may purse his lips, turn his head away from the food, or push the spoon away. If your baby begins to play with the food or spoon or becomes restless, this can be a cue that he's no longer hungry and it's time for mealtime to come to an end. Narrate what you see. "You dropped the spoon on the floor." "You're closing your lips." "You're wiggling. It looks like you're all done."

▪ If your baby seems thirsty and you'd like to give him some water, offer it from a clear glass. Pour a small amount—about one-half inch—of water from the pitcher into the drinking glass. Hold the glass from the bottom so that your baby can grasp the sides of the glass if he'd like to. Touch the glass to your baby's lower lip and wait for him to open his mouth. Tilt the glass slightly so that he takes in just a small amount of liquid.

▪ When your baby lets you know that he's finished eating and drinking, it's time to wash his face and hands and take off his bib. At this point, he may be squirming and ready to rest or get back to playing. Try your best not to hurry. Ask for his cooperation. Picking up the washcloth, you might say, "I'd like to wash your hands. May I have this hand? How about your other one? I'd like to wipe your mouth. Let's take off your bib."

Feeding from a Folding Tray Table

Once your baby can get into a sitting position on his own, you can use a breakfast-in-bed tray on the floor for feeding. It's sometimes easiest to make this transition by starting with your baby seated in your lap in front of the table. Let your baby eat this way for a few days or longer, and when he seems comfortable, he can transition to sitting in front of the table on the floor, with you sitting beside or opposite him. Some parents are convinced that their baby will crawl away from the table and never eat. But if your baby is hungry, and if limits are clearly articulated, he can quickly learn that he needs to stay at the table to eat, or else the food will be put away. Remember the RIE principle to trust in your baby's competence! Here's how to feed your baby at a tray table:

- If you like, lay a mat on the floor for easy cleanup, with the folding tray table on top of it.

- Beside that, place a tray with a damp washcloth, bib, serving bowl of food and serving spoon, feeding bowl, two feeding spoons (or forks, depending on the food), drinking glass, and pitcher of water or other liquid. If you're offering finger food, place the food in a serving bowl from which you can take a few pieces at a time, and place them directly on the table for the child to pick up.

- Once you've invited your baby to the table, and when first introducing eating at the tray table, narrate your expectations. "We're going to sit here together while you eat." If your baby is sitting next to you rather than on your lap, you can touch the mat to indicate where you'd like him to sit. "You can sit here on the mat."

- Start by washing your baby's hands with the washcloth and putting on his bib.

- If you're feeding from a spoon, put the bowl of food on the table and take the food from there. As when you were lap feeding, if your baby wants to take the utensil to feed himself, let him do so. Until he's mastered using it, he may choose to eat with his hands when he's really hungry. When he's ready and with practice, he'll learn to use a spoon or fork with confidence and ease. Forcing him to do so before he is ready may only lead to frustration and upset.

- If you're offering small, bite-size finger foods, start by placing just a couple of pieces on the tray for your baby to pick up with his fingers. He will let you know when he wants more, and then you can put down a couple more pieces. When we overload a table or dish with too much food, we send an unconscious message about how much we expect a baby to eat. If you offer just a little, then your baby can tune in to himself to know when he's had enough. This is also an opportunity to develop trust between parent and baby. The baby asks for more food, and the attentive parent provides it.

- When your baby indicates that he is done, it's time to wash his hands and face and take off his bib. Then he can move away from the table on his own. If he begins to play with the food or come and go from the table, you can tell him that it seems as if he's no longer interested in eating, so you're going to put the food away.

When you first introduce the tray table, your baby may try to crawl onto it to explore—it may be necessary to set clear limits, particularly in the beginning. Your baby may also crawl to and from the table for the first couple of days as he gets used to this new eating arrangement. You may say, "I want you to stay here while you're eating." But on the second or third day, if he crawls away again, you might say, "When you crawl away from the table, it tells me you're not hungry." If he moves away yet again, you can set a limit by saying, "You crawled away from the table. It looks like you're all done, so I'm going to put away the food." Carry through by slowly getting up and putting the food away. Fold up the tray table and mat and stow them away. This provides a visual signal that the kitchen is now closed. You are doing this not to punish but to set clear limits. Your baby may protest, but chances are good that very quickly he'll learn that when he moves away from the table, the food disappears. He'll come to understand the limit and, if he's hungry, will stay at the table with you until his hunger is satiated. Once he's walking and graduates to a table and stool, the "staying seated while eating" limit remains the same. Yours will not be a toddler who wanders around the house with food in one hand and cup in the other. Believe it or not, it *is* possible to have a pleasurable and dignified meal with a baby or toddler, but we have to patiently set clear and consistent limits and be willing to follow through with them to achieve this goal.

In Parent-Infant Guidance classes, once all the babies are able to sit up on their own, we offer them a snack of banana and water. I talk to the parents ahead of time about the routine—if a child is interested in having a snack, he must have his hands washed, wear a bib, and remain seated. Pretty simple, right? Although these are the "house rules," I don't have any expectation that the babies will adhere to them quickly or easily. It may take many weeks, if not months, for a baby to internalize the limits and no longer require me to gently remind him of the house rules. Some babies and toddlers choose never to participate in the snack, which is perfectly acceptable as well. Parents often doubt that their baby will be willing to follow the rules, but to their joy and amazement, they soon discover their baby's willingness and competency. My guess is that the babies know my limits are nonnegotiable. If they're hungry, they learn to dine in accordance with the guidelines I set.

Using RIE principles with my nine-month-old son — setting aside time for his meal, sitting with him on the floor at a low table, using a small glass tumbler or little cup instead of a plastic sippy cup — means that I have to slow down, stay present, and attentive. My little boy is more present at meals because I'm completely there for him, rather than running around the kitchen doing other things. Mealtimes are slower, calmer, and more of a sacred time, giving me the opportunity to focus on and connect with the little person in front of me. At first my son cried when I insisted that he sit down to eat and drink. But by the third time, he got it and seemed proud to be competent in this way. While the high chair (which I do sometimes use) offers external reassurance and security, sitting at the low table allows him the freedom to get up when he decides he's finished eating.

I used the same approach with my older child, now a toddler, and the payoff is clear: she sits and participates at mealtimes. She's proud to model for her brother and show him how to sit and eat. She becomes excited when she can help her brother by offering him bits of food or help him with his bib.

— Alexandra Blaker

Feeding at a Small Table and a Stool

Once a toddler is walking confidently, it's time to introduce a small stool and toddler-size table for mealtimes. At RIE, we use a round, stable stool because it's easier to negotiate than a chair, since it can be approached from any direction, and a child can sit securely with his feet on the floor. A chair adds an extra layer of complexity that a young toddler may not yet be ready for. It can also be unsafe if a child grasps the back of the chair and puts his weight on it. A stool also allows a toddler to get up on his own when he is finished, rather than waiting for someone to free him from a high chair.

▪ If you like, place a mat on the floor for easy cleanup, with the table on top of it. If he's interested, your toddler can assist you with the preparations by pulling out his stool and getting his bib and utensils out of a low cupboard. If you're setting up yourself, next to the table, on a tray or in a bin, place a damp washcloth, bib, serving bowl of food and serving spoon, feeding bowl or plate, two feeding spoons, drinking glass, and pitcher of water or other liquid.

▪ Before eating, it's time to wash and dry hands. Young toddlers may need your assistance; older toddlers may be able to successfully accomplish this on their own. Hand washing can happen at the sink or at the table with a washcloth. Just put on a bib, and it's time to eat.

▪ Narrate. At snack time, we might say to a toddler, "I know you're hungry. Would you like to take your stool to the table, or shall I? [Child carries stool or slides it to table and sits down.] Let's wash your hands. [Child presents hands to be washed.] Which bib would you like? The blue or the green? [Child points to bib.] Are you ready to put on your bib? [Child leans head forward for bib.] [Fastening bib.] There you go. [Showing child two bowls of food.] Would you like cheese or apple? [Child points to apple.] [Offering a piece of apple.]"

▪ Moving slowly creates a sense of calm and helps the child tune in to his sensations of hunger and satiation. At Parent-Infant Guidance classes, when a toddler is bouncing up and down on his stool, loudly demanding more, I slow down—not to torture the child but to model patience and peacefulness. The child invariably calms and learns to wait more patiently for his food.

▪ If you're offering small, bite-size finger foods, start by placing just a couple of pieces on the table or plate for the child to pick up with his fingers. He'll let you know when he'd like more, and then you can put a couple more pieces down for him to pick up. Remember not to put too much food down at one time, and wait until the child asks before offering more. If you're offering cereal, pasta, or food from a bowl, place the bowl on the table and take the food from there. Whenever your toddler shows interest in feeding himself, let him do so.

▪ If he wants something to drink, you can offer your toddler liquid in a small, clear glass. At RIE, we give young toddlers the opportunity to pour their own water. We pour about one-half inch of water from a serving pitcher into a small, clear glass pitcher and place the pitcher on the table in front of the child so that he can do the pouring. At first he may try to drink from the pitcher, but he will quickly learn that the pitcher is for pouring. Is it sometimes messier than the adult doing the pouring? Absolutely. But the child takes such pleasure in this simple task and his budding independence. It also provides an opportunity for fine motor activity.

When people visit our center, they are often amazed to see pretoddlers pouring their own milk and want to know how we taught the children to do that. We don't need to "teach" the children how to pour. We create an environment that fosters competence and self-help skills, and they learn to do it themselves.

— Polly Elam, RIE Associate

- When your child shows you that he's done, it's time to wash his hands and face. He may want to do this himself with you assisting here and there, just to finish up the spots he missed. Then it's time for him to take off his bib.

- After cleaning himself up, your toddler may want to help bring the dishes to the kitchen or wipe the table with a sponge. Let him do things to the best of his ability and refrain from correcting or instructing him.

When you invite your baby to participate in his care, you're letting him know that you value his participation. As he learns to take on more and more of his self-care, he takes pleasure in his growing ability, and this supports his emerging self-confidence and self-reliance. Caregiving forms a large part of your baby's "curriculum," so take time to enjoy these special moments together.

4. Sleep

Your goal is to help your baby develop good sleep habits.... The easiest way to develop good habits in general is to have a predictable daily life.
—Magda Gerber, *Dear Parent*

All of us need to sleep, but it's especially important for babies, who need many hours of uninterrupted sleep for their physical, cognitive, and emotional development. Rested babies learn and process information more readily than babies who don't get enough sleep. A tired baby will be irritable and unable to focus. Depending on her age, she may be listless or hyperactive. It's important for parents to do what they can to protect their baby's sleep, not only for their baby's health and well-being but for the happiness of the entire family.

When I teach RIE's Before Baby course to expectant parents and we talk about sleep, I start by asking the parents how they go to sleep each night. How do you fall asleep at night? Do you sleep on your back, your stomach, or your side? Are you comfortable with just one pillow, or do you prefer several—under your head, between your knees, next to your stomach? If you wake in the middle of the night, how do you get back to sleep? It soon becomes clear that no one goes to sleep the same way or in the same amount of time. And no one can make anyone else go to sleep.

The same is true for babies. Although you can't teach your baby to sleep, you *can* create an atmosphere that is conducive to rest, one that is peaceful and quiet, in which your baby can develop good sleep habits. You can respond to your baby in ways that will help her to recognize when she is tired, learn to self-soothe and get to sleep on her own, and look forward to rest. You can convey an attitude about sleep that sends the message that rest is pleasurable and that her bed is a cozy, comfortable place to be. Of course, there will be times when sleep may be more of a challenge—when your baby is sick, over-tired, or overstimulated. But your attitude about sleep and the routines you establish will serve you well during these more difficult times.

HOW BABIES SLEEP

Each baby is different when it comes to when and how long she sleeps. If only babies arrived with warranties that promised they would sleep for twelve hours at night and stay awake during the day! Newborn babies, however, fall asleep at any time of the day or night, wake up to be fed, and then go back to sleep again, caring little for the routines of the rest of the world. Both the amount and the pattern of sleep vary from child to child and change as a baby grows.

A newborn baby's sleep pattern, especially during the first month to six weeks, is unpredictable. In those first weeks, babies sleep most of the time, alternating periods of sleep and wakefulness six to ten times during one twenty-four-hour period. They wake every two to four hours for a feeding, day and night. Their schedules may be entirely upside down, with more sleep happening during the day than at night. This is because their circadian rhythm—or twenty-four-hour sleep-wake cycle—has not yet developed. To help your baby establish her sleep rhythm, expose her to natural light and sound during the day, and as the day winds down, try your best to create an atmosphere that is darker and quieter. She will begin to understand cues for sleep and waking from her environment and attune to her body's signals of tiredness. Protecting your baby's sleep schedule will strengthen her circadian rhythm, support healthy sleep habits, and ensure that she gets quality, restorative sleep when she needs it.

Within a few months, you can expect your baby's sleep patterns to be more consistent. She'll likely fall asleep around the same time every evening and wake up around the same time every morning. She may need a feeding or two during the night but will usually fall right back to sleep. Eventually night-time feedings will likely no longer be necessary. How can you tell? Observe your baby. When she cries during the night and seeks your attention, does she seem hungry, or is she asking for or demanding reassurance and assistance to settle back down to sleep? If she is more interested in engaging with you than in feeding, this nighttime meeting is not about hunger.

You can help your baby to change this habit and encourage her to go back to sleep on her own during the night. Before bed-time, talk to your baby about how tonight is going to be differ-ent. Let her know that if she wakes in the night, you want her to go back to sleep. If she wakes and cries, don't rush in to her. Instead wait, and then wait a little longer to see if she can settle back to sleep on her own. If someone needs to go in, it may be best for the father or the parent who has not been doing the nighttime feedings to go in during this period of adjustment because baby hasn't come to expect middle-of-the-night feed-ings from this parent. Whether it's the father, mother, or another caregiver, be as boring as possible and do as little as pos-sible, starting with the smallest intervention first. Rather than immediately picking up your baby and taking her out of the crib to calm her, see if a few gentle strokes on her back will be enough to soothe her. Sometimes just having you nearby to offer emo-tional support is enough. The less you do, the more she will rely on herself to find a way to calm and settle back to sleep.

HOW TO TELL WHEN YOUR BABY IS TIRED

In the first few months of life, babies will generally sleep as much as they need to. As they become more alert and social, they often begin to resist sleep. At this point, parents can, for better or worse, influence their baby's emerging sleep pattern. The goal is for babies to become attuned to their natural sleep-wake rhythms and for adults to provide the opportunity and place for babies to rest when they're tired.

We value sleep, know it's important, and do what we can to protect sleep time for the baby. This sounds simple, but how can you tell when your baby is tired? Start by observing to see if you can notice the "soft signs" of tiredness:

- She rubs or closes her eyes.
- She slows down or moves less competently.
- She becomes still and quiet.
- She no longer engages with play objects.
- She seems less focused or stares off into space.
- She sucks her thumb, fingers, or hand.
- A toddler becomes aggressive by hitting or biting.

Once you've become adept at identifying these *soft* signs of tiredness, see if you can notice what happens just *before* these signs appear. Sometimes, by the time your baby is rubbing her eyes, she's actually *over*tired and well on her way to becoming irritable. It can then be difficult for her to settle down to sleep easily. Before she is rubbing her eyes, she may seek you out or want to be held. Toddlers can be particularly tricky to read. A toddler who appears to be full of energy may instead be "wired" and overtired. She may yell or be giddy and giggle uncontrollably. She may behave aggressively by pushing or hitting. Learning to observe and notice sleepiness cues takes time and practice.

As your baby grows and becomes more alert and aware of her surroundings, she may become more resistant to sleep — and once the "second wind" hits, going to sleep can become an ordeal for both of you. An overtired baby sleeps restlessly, wakes up more frequently during the night, and is often irritable and unhappy the next day. Just like her parents.

WHERE AND WHEN TO SLEEP

Lay your baby down to sleep in the same place each time, whether it's a bassinet, a crib, or a bed. Magda believed that babies could benefit from sleeping in their own crib but always asked parents what worked best for them. She said that sleeping in a crib "is a way of learning togetherness and separateness, and that separateness is not the same as abandonment. A child sleeping in her own bed still knows that if she cries or if something happens, her parents will be there."[1] Many of the families in my classes co-sleep with their babies. Where your baby sleeps is a personal decision, one that differs from family to family and from culture to culture. The same principles apply no matter where your baby sleeps, as long as the place is safe for your baby's sleeping. If you look at your baby's crib or bed as a comfortable and cozy place for rest, chances are your baby will come to feel this way too.

Babies and toddlers should not be put to sleep in car seats, swings, bouncy seats, or other contraptions. These devices will certainly render your baby immobile and may lull her to sleep, but they are not intended for sleeping. In fact, they will prevent your baby from getting good quality sleep. Do you feel as rested when you fall asleep in a chair or on a plane as when you sleep flat on your own bed? Lay your baby down to sleep flat on her back in her crib, so that she has room to move and to roll over when she is able to do so. Since 1992, the American Academy of Pediatrics has recommended that babies be laid on their backs to sleep to reduce the risk of sudden infant death syndrome (SIDS).

When the sleep environment is spare and simple, your baby can more easily tune in to her body and her own inner rhythms. A mobile may seem cute and pretty to an adult but can be a distraction for your baby. Would you want something dangling overhead and playing a tinny song as you were trying to nod off to sleep? Let your baby tune in to her own body, and don't distract her from rest with sleep-inducing devices. Trust that she can learn to go to sleep without interventions, and give her time to figure things out on her own. Keep the crib free of stuffed animals and play objects so that your baby can focus on sleeping. An older baby or toddler may have a precious stuffed animal or lovey blanket that she uses as her transitional object. She may use it for comfort at nap time or bedtime and at other times as well.

Everything that happens to your baby during the day influences her sleep patterns. The first step to developing good sleep habits is for your baby's day to be relaxed and predictable. It will probably be easier for your baby to go to sleep after a day that peacefully rolls along than after a day that has her in and out of a car seat, with a lot of interruptions, noise, and other distractions. Many of us lead busy lives, and we can't shelter our babies from all of it. But we can endeavor to keep our baby's lives as simple as possible.

Some babies develop fairly consistent sleep schedules within a few months, and others continue to sleep at varying times for much longer. In either case, it's important to look to your baby for signs of tiredness and lay her down to sleep then. By observing your baby, you will notice patterns begin to emerge, and know that she may likely tire around the same times each day. As your baby grows and develops, her daytime sleep schedule will shift, but once established, her nighttime sleep schedule will remain fairly consistent. Creating and following a regular sleep routine will support your baby in developing healthy sleep habits.

BEDTIME ROUTINE

When it's time to rest, for a nap or at night, move slowly, talk quietly, and create an atmosphere of calm and peacefulness. According to one study, "parents' emotional availability at bedtimes may be as important, if not more important, than bedtime practices in predicting infant sleep quality."[2] So slow yourself down and gaze into your baby's eyes as you quietly talk to her. If she is very tired, she may not want to make eye contact but may prefer to stare off into space. Let it be her choice. This is a time to give your attention to your baby and attune to her cues and rhythms. By doing this, you will create a feeling of safety and warmth around your child that will help her welcome the sleep that is to come. Making an emotional connection with your child before leaving her on her own to rest is important for all children but may be particularly important for working parents. By taking the time to be fully present with your baby in the moments before rest, you can refuel your child emotionally so that she can let go of you to sleep. Of course, if there are siblings in the house, this can be a challenge. Do your best to help other children understand that their baby brother or sister needs quiet at bedtime.

Routines for going to sleep at nap time and nighttime are important, and following a slow pace for each can help your baby learn how to progress calmly toward sleep. The routine is yours to create; simple and relatively brief are preferable to long and drawn out. A bath before nighttime can relax your baby—although it may have an energizing effect for some. After the bath, you might read a short book to your baby and say good night to the stuffed animals. Then it's time to lay your baby in her crib. You can narrate what you're doing before you leave the room. "I'm pulling down the shade. I'm turning on your night-light. Now I'm turning off the lamp. I'm going to the kitchen. Have a wonderful rest. I'll see you in the morning." Whatever your routine, if you follow the same steps each time, your baby will learn to anticipate what comes next.

With an older baby or toddler, you can talk about what she's done that day and what will happen the following day. This provides a sense of continuity that one day naturally flows into the next, and can help to ease any nighttime anxieties. When the bedtime ritual has a predictable rhythm, your child can relax and learn to welcome sleep peacefully and without difficulty. Let your voice and gestures express what a true pleasure it is to sleep.

If two parents want to participate in the nighttime routine, notice if this overstimulates your baby. It may be that three's a crowd. Your baby may tolerate one of you saying good night and leaving the room, but two at a time may be too much. In this case, one parent may want to say good night before a book is read. Perhaps one parent can lead the nighttime routine during the week and the other on the weekend. If you wonder how best to proceed, observe your baby. What riles her up, and what routine helps her to settle down most easily?

Do your best to lay your baby down to rest while she is still awake. Then later, when she wakes in her crib, she won't be surprised or disoriented because she'll remember how she got there. This can be difficult to accomplish with your newborn baby, who may nod off in your arms while nursing or having a bottle. As she grows, laying her down while still awake will be a lot easier. If it's not, start the routine earlier the next night, so that the final step of the routine finishes before she becomes overtired. This is important because you don't want your baby to associate sleeping with feeding, learning that she needs to eat to fall asleep. Hunger and sleep are two separate needs. If you've ever found yourself in front of the fridge late at night in a daze and realized that you're not hungry but tired, you know what I mean. We all need sleep at night to refuel, not food.

WHEN BABY CRIES . . . WAIT

The minutes between when a baby is laid down to rest and when she falls asleep often produce anxiety for parents. They wait and listen nervously, wondering if their baby will get to sleep on her own. They worry that she'll cry. If she *does* cry, they quickly go back into the room to pick her up and comfort her. With the best of intentions, they can create a habit and a dependency. A 2002 study found that "the children of parents who waited longer to respond to their [baby's] awakenings at three months were more likely to be self-soothers by 12 months of age."[3] What does this mean? Parents who pause and wait a little longer before responding to their baby's crying give their babies the opportunity to develop self-soothing skills.

So if you've laid your baby in her crib and she begins to cry, before you rush in, pause, take a breath, wait, and then wait a little longer. Listen to your baby. What does this particular cry sound like? Is it a rhythmic whimper? Does it start and stop? Is this cry different from other cries? Remember that crying is your baby's *language*, the way she expresses her feelings and needs. You can't learn a new language immediately, so give yourself time to listen and learn the cries in your baby's unique repertoire. Maybe she whimpers to self-soothe. Perhaps she *needs* to cry for a while to release the day's tensions before she finally relaxes into sleep. Now take a moment to observe yourself. Are you feeling anxious? Angry? Are you holding your breath? Say what you're feeling aloud. Speak to yourself. "She's crying. I feel anxious. I want to go in and pick her up. That would certainly make *me* feel better. But I also want to give her time to see what she can do on her own. Even though she's crying, I don't want to assume she needs me. Maybe she's crying to settle herself to sleep. I don't want to interrupt her, so I'll wait another minute to see what happens."

Narrating for yourself can slow you down and ease your tension. Of course, if your baby's crying is ramping up and she's sounding distressed, then by all means, go into her room to reassure her. It's best to go to her before she's so overwrought that she needs a lot of help to calm. Once your baby is flooded with cortisol, the hormone that is released during stress, it's likely she will need your help to lower her stress and to calm. Unfortunately there's no perfect science that tells us when to intervene and how. But through careful listening and observation, we can become sensitively attuned to our babies and respond more accurately to their needs.

If you do go back into the room to comfort your baby, start with the smallest step first. Enter the room slowly and quietly. Remember that your baby will pick up on your emotions, so be careful not to convey a "poor you" attitude. There's no pre-scribed script for you to follow, but here's an example of what you might do. Go over to your baby's crib and slowly and gently stroke her chest, just once. Quietly say, "I hear you. It's time to rest now." Stand there quietly for a moment. See if your words and touch have helped her to calm. Notice her breathing and then notice your own. Are you feeling tense? If you are, take a deep breath. Try to relax. Continue observing your baby. If she seems to need more soothing, slowly and gently stroke her chest again. Are words necessary this time? Perhaps your gentle touch will offer enough comfort that she'll be able to close her eyes and rest. Or maybe just sitting in a chair in the room with her will provide the needed reassurance. There is no one right answer for all babies and all situations, but the rule of thumb is to try to do as little as possible, as quietly and peacefully as possible. Less is more.

Toddlers can be highly creative with their stalling tactics. After you say good night and leave the room, they may sud-denly be thirsty, hungry, or have something very important to tell you that absolutely can't wait until the morning. They can beg you for just one more story. Creating good sleep habits involves setting limits, and limits can best be set well before bedtime. Before brushing teeth, you may say, "If you're thirsty, let's get you a drink. This is your last drink until morning." Give a gentle reminder that although you love to hear what your child has to tell you, once you say good night, all conversation has to wait until the morning. Instead of pointing to a shelf full of books and asking your child to choose, pull out just a few and let her pick one or two from among them. Let your child know you're setting these limits because you care about her and sleep is important to both of you.

Parents play a huge role in creating healthy sleep habits by establishing and following through with a consistent prebedtime routine. Your baby needs long periods of uninterrupted sleep for brain growth and physical development. Of course, young babies wake up for feedings every few hours, and children who have colds or other illnesses can be too uncomfortable to sleep well and may need more attention than usual. When children are reaching physical and cognitive milestones, they're more likely to wake in the night. They may need extra reassurance during significant transitions such as a new child care situation or when traveling away from home. Starting babies off with a consistent, early evening routine will help to establish healthy sleep habits for a lifetime.

NO TRICKS NECESSARY

Many weary parents resort to a bag of tricks — excessive rocking, carrying the baby around, long drives in the car, or even naps on top of a humming dryer — until their baby falls asleep. These interventions work because the baby's movement is restricted, so what can she do but go to sleep? But sleep in a contraption or moving vehicle is not good quality sleep, and these interventions prevent the baby from practicing and perfecting getting to sleep on her own. They can even have a hypnotic effect. Your baby will quickly become accustomed to whatever you do with her. An intervention may offer a quick fix in the moment, but you won't want to drive her around in the car or rock her excessively each time she needs to sleep. What provided a speedy solution last week can introduce a new set of issues the next. Perhaps your baby has learned to be rocked to sleep but now wakes when you transfer her to the crib. By refraining from being the one to "get your baby to sleep," you will give your baby an early opportunity to learn to find her way to sleep on her own.

When Cy was four to six months old, he had trouble settling down for naps. We tried to help him by singing a song (or five), standing and rocking with him, walking around his room, sometimes for half an hour. When we put him down, he continued to cry. We checked on him every few minutes, but it was such an ordeal for all of us trying to help him sleep! One afternoon, I got the sense that Cy just wanted to be put down in his crib and left alone, so that's what I did. He fell asleep easily and quickly. Aha! Cy was trying to tell us that we were doing too much. Now we have a simple nap time routine — no rocking — and he has become a great napper.

— Bianca Siegl

When it comes to sleep, remember a basic Educaring tenet: Trust in your infant's competence. Learning to self-soothe and go to sleep on her own doesn't happen overnight, so give your baby the time she needs to learn this important skill.

Trust that your baby is competent enough to learn this and know that you're nearby, attentive and supportive, but ultimately it is up to your baby to discover how to go to sleep. *Baby knows best!*

NAPS

A good night's sleep is not enough. Daytime sleep is essential to your baby's health and happiness. In the first few months of your baby's life, her naps may vary widely, both in timing and in duration. After a few months, she will transition to two or three naps a day, with the first nap taking place about one and a half hours after she wakes in the morning. Eventually she'll drop the third nap, and later still you'll notice that her morning nap is moving later and later or is really more of a catnap. This can signal that she's ready to consolidate to just one nap a day, beginning midday or early afternoon and lasting from an hour and a half to as long as three hours. The transition from two naps a day to one can take weeks to complete and can be confusing. One day she may need just one nap and the next day two. Today she may be ready to nap at noon, and tomorrow it may be 1:00. Observing your baby for signs of tiredness will serve you well during this time of change.

Some babies are so ready for rest that they reach toward their crib in anticipation and need no prenap routine at all. Or your baby may enjoy looking at a book with you, and this can help to ease the transition toward a nap. It may be difficult to have a quiet home during the day; you may be busy with other children, work, or household chores. Although it may not be a time to blast music or practice your tap dancing, it's fine if the phone rings or someone knocks on the door. We can't expect the world to be quiet when our babies are napping, so don't be overly concerned with background noises during the day. Your baby can learn to sleep through them.

NIGHTTIME WAKING

If your baby wakes to feed in the middle of the night, be as boring and understimulating as possible. Let your behavior convey that you're there to fulfill her need for food but it's not playtime. Offer the bottle or breast quietly. Is talking necessary? Probably not. Does the diaper need to be changed? Not necessarily. If you can nurse or offer a bottle by the light of the night-light, that's preferable to brightening the room by turning on a light. In other words, let the environment cue your baby that although she may be hungry and need nourishment, it's *not* time to start the day.

Learning to recognize the difference between an anxious or distressed cry and a protest cry will help you to figure out how to respond to your baby in the middle of the night. Remember that the ultimate goal is for your baby to learn to go to sleep on her own and self-soothe when she wakes in the night, so the less you do, the better. Just like all things your baby will learn, self-soothing takes practice and may involve a certain amount of struggle. If you can accept that struggle is a natural part of the process—indeed, of life—you will be more likely to wait, then wait another minute, to allow your baby to find her way to sleep.

Eventually your baby will no longer need to feed in the middle of the night. If she has not relied on you or some other external device to get to sleep, she will more easily move between lighter and deeper sleep on her own throughout the night. If you always rock your baby to sleep before putting her in her crib, waking up alone in the middle of the night may alarm her. If she routinely uses a pacifier to settle herself and wakes in the middle of the night without it, she may cry until you appear to find it and put it back in her mouth (and it may fall out again five minutes later). The habits your baby relies on to get to sleep at the beginning of the night will be the same ones she will turn to at 3:00 a.m.

If your toddler is waking you in the middle of the night, talk to her well before bedtime about how tonight is going to be different, everybody in the family needs to get a good night's sleep, you'll be resting in your room, she'll be safe and cozy in her bed, and you'll come in to see her when it's morning. If she wakes and wails at the gate of her bedroom or pads down to yours, return her to her bed. Children's healthy sleep habits are largely determined by parental attitude, emotional state, and resolve.

GETTING ENOUGH SLEEP

Making sure your baby gets enough of the right kind of deep, restorative sleep is as important as her learning to fall asleep on her own. I suggest to parents who attend RIE Parent-Infant Guidance class that if their baby is tired, they should lay her down to sleep as early as 6:00 or 6:30 at night. This often comes as a shock:

"I won't have any time to play with her after not seeing her all day!"

"But I don't pick her up from day care until 5:00 p.m."

"If I put her to bed at 6:00, won't she wake up at 4:00?"

Parents are often surprised to learn that keeping a baby up later will not cause her to sleep later the next day; in fact, the opposite is often true. Dr. Marc Weissbluth says, "An earlier bedtime will allow your child to sleep later, just as a too-late bedtime will eventually cause a too-early wake-up time. Remember that sleep begets sleep. This is not logical, but it is biological."[4] Although it may seem counterintuitive, putting your baby to bed *earlier* may help her to sleep later in the morning and to sleep well at night. Likewise, waking up a baby from her nap or cutting it out altogether to try to get her to sleep better at night can make nighttime sleep even more difficult.

Particularly for working parents, an early bedtime may sound easier said than done. If you don't pick your baby up from child care until 6:00, it won't be possible for her to be in bed by 6:30, but do what you can to provide as early a bedtime as possible. Baths don't necessarily have to happen in the evening, so this is one way to shorten the evening routine.

When Leslie brought her glassy-eyed and listless eight-month-old daughter, Olivia, to Parent-Infant Guidance class, I asked about her sleep schedule. She said that she and her husband, Michael, routinely put Olivia to bed at 8:30 p.m. Michael didn't get home from work until 7:00, and he treasured this precious time with his daughter. They kept to the same schedule on the weekends. As we observed the babies that day, Leslie could clearly see that Olivia didn't engage with the play objects and interact with other babies the way the other children did. She was just plain tired. Leslie and Michael made a commitment to change their schedules so that Olivia could go to sleep at 6:30

each night. They changed their own sleep schedules, too, going to bed by 10:00 and getting up at 5:30. With this new schedule, Olivia was asleep by the time Michael got home from work. But when she woke at 6:00 a.m., Michael and his well-rested daughter had an hour and a half together before Michael had to leave at 7:30. Did the schedule happen overnight? No. Did it require Leslie and Michael to make some initial sacrifices? Yes. But they were rewarded with a well-rested baby, who seemed so different from the tired baby they'd known before. A few months after this new schedule had been established, we were observing the babies in class. Leslie shared her observations of Olivia and how her movements and interactions with the other babies were now so different since making changes to the family's sleep schedules. She confessed that they just hadn't realized that Olivia had been chronically overtired. Leslie and Michael found a solution that worked for their family.

ILLNESS

When your baby is sick, she'll need you to comfort her more. She may want to be held in your arms and generally want more of your attention. Her ability to self-soothe may be reduced, so she may rely on you more than usual. If she has been in the habit of sleeping through the night, when she's sick, she may need you if she wakes and is uncomfortable. Don't be concerned. Observe and offer your baby what you think she needs in the moment, and know that when she's feeling better, you'll both be able to get the routine and schedule back on track. It may take some time to return to your previous routines, but having the resolve to get there will make all the difference.

VACATIONS

Since predictability is an important part of healthy sleep habits, keep to your bedtime routine and schedule as much as possible when you and your baby are away from home and she is sleeping in an unfamiliar place. If she has a beloved blanket or play object, be sure to bring it with you. For example, if you go to Grandma's house, familiarize your baby with her new environment as soon as you arrive and well before bedtime. Spend some time in the bedroom together. Show your baby where she'll be sleeping. Tell her how you'll close the curtains and lower the lights just as you do at home. As always, your attitude will convey a lot to your baby about this new experience. If you're feeling confident and at ease, your baby will pick up on this, and sleeping at Grandma's will feel much like sleeping at home.

If you're traveling to a different time zone, put your baby to rest at the appropriate time in this new location. In other words, if her usual bedtime is 7:00 p.m., lay her down when it's 7:00 p.m. in your new location, not when it's 7:00 p.m. at home. Your baby may surprise you by needing a restorative nap at what seems to be an odd time, so make sure to observe her for signs of tiredness. When you return home, do the same by adjusting her schedule back to local time.

FROM CRIB TO BED

When should your baby transition from a crib to a bed? Many parents make the move when their toddler has climbed and fallen out of her crib. Other families make the change when a new baby is on the way. In this case, it's wise to begin the transition process several months before the new baby is due. Having a new sleeping place and a new sibling all at once is too much for most children to endure.

Generally speaking, most toddlers will transition to a bed sometime between two and three years old. But wait until your child is sleeping well before you consider transitioning her to a bed. Doing this in two steps can help things to go more smoothly. You might start by moving her from her crib to a mattress on the floor. This way, no one need be concerned about her falling out of bed. When your child is comfortable with this and has done it successfully for at least a few weeks, you can then transition her to a bed. If you don't want to put a mattress on the floor, a bed rail may provide additional safety and security until your child gets used to sleeping in her new bed.

As always, it's important to talk to your child about her new bed. Now that she's no longer in her crib, some limits may need to be reinforced. "Tonight you'll sleep in your new bed in your room. It's comfy and cozy, and you can cuddle with Teddy. I want you to stay in your bed until morning." Talking about the change and asking your child if she has any questions can help you discover any anxieties she might have about her sleeping arrangement. Your calm attitude can help to convey that this is a natural transition, one that you know she is ready to make successfully and easily. If your child pops up and comes out of her room, calmly and gently bring her back in and tell her that she needs to stay in her bed to rest. Installing a gate at the door to her room before she even begins to crawl can help to make the transition to a bed a lot easier because boundaries will already have been established.

* * *

Parents are understandably eager for their babies to sleep through the night so that the entire family can get a full night of rest. The less you do to "help" your baby to sleep, the sooner she will learn to get to and stay asleep on her own. If she begins to cry once you've laid her down or when she no longer needs feeding in the middle of the night, pause and observe to see if she can settle on her own rather than rushing in and picking her up. Establish a bedtime routine and give your baby time to acquire skills such as self-soothing and falling asleep on her own. You will soon notice just how competent she can be.

5. Free to Move

*Every baby moves with more ease and efficiency if
allowed to do it at his own time and in his own way,
without our trying to teach him.*
—Magda Gerber, *Dear Parent*

Is Kiara crawling yet?"

"How old is Lily? Really, and she's not walking?"

A lot of attention is paid to babies reaching milestones such as rolling over, crawling, sitting up, standing, and walking. Parents sometimes become anxious if their babies haven't achieved these milestones by a certain age. But before a baby is able to sit, stand, or walk, he has to figure out how to find balance in each incremental position that will prepare him to reach the next major milestone. Before he intentionally rolls over onto his tummy, he will practice balancing on his side. Before he is able to sit or stand, he must first learn to balance with more and more of his body off the ground until he's finally able to support his weight in the upright, standing position. It can take a lot of practice for a parent to learn to relax and appreciate what a baby *is* doing rather than worry about a milestone he has yet to reach. Magda asked, "Why is it so difficult to accept the importance of readiness? Normally developing children do what they can do; they do not withhold. Parents who expect their children to perform on a level the child has not yet reached are creating failure and disappointment for both the children and themselves. Don't people realize how it possibly affects young children when what they can do is not appreciated but what they cannot do is expected?"[1]

When working in group care one year, we had only one child at the start…and what a child: he was a total joy to be around. He smiled and cooed, went to sleep peacefully and easily, played happily on the floor....Basically, he was just an all-round "easy" baby. As he got a little older, I started to wonder when he would roll over. He seemed to be interested: He'd look at nearby toys and sometimes grab for them, arching his back a bit and twisting; but if he couldn't reach, he'd happily just relax onto his back and smile at the ceiling. I tell people that this was my true test in my trust of children's natural abilities....I thought, "Wouldn't you know it? I have the opportunity to really watch a child learn to roll over, and I've got this guy who is so happy on his back, happy not to roll over....He's going to just grow longer and longer, and before you know it, he'll just get up off the floor and walk into kindergarten without ever rolling over!" But as the days passed, I started to notice him getting a little fussy at times: He *wasn't* that same content child who would lie peacefully on the floor. He cried, he squirmed, he scrunched up his body, and even when I picked him up, he'd reach back toward the floor. I wondered, was he hungry? No. Was he sleepy? No. Did he need a diaper? No. What's going on? Well, after just a few days of this fussiness, he rolled over! Aha! Something inside him told him it was time, and he did it!

— Melani Ladygo, RIE Associate

As Magda noted, babies are born knowing how to move; they don't need to be taught. They move and kick in utero and continue to move as soon as they are born. Movement is so instinctual that if a newborn is laid on the mother's tummy, he will migrate toward the breast. Fine motor (the muscles in the hands and fingers) and gross motor (the large muscle groups of the neck, trunk, arms, and legs) development happens naturally. Babies will hold up their heads, turn onto their tummies, crawl, and walk when they are ready. They take pleasure in movement and learn to move without adult assistance or instruction.

Many parents believe they need to exercise their babies or teach them how to crawl down stairs or walk. But the way your baby moves naturally is always the best and safest way for him to move. Many times, I've seen a baby begin to crawl down stairs headfirst, and then an adult comes in, turns the baby around, and instructs him to go down feet first. I watched a friend repeat this direction over and over again, and each time her baby proceeded to crawl down the steps, facing forward. Going down headfirst makes perfect sense. The baby can see where he's going!

Imagine you were getting on your bike to go for a ride and a friend said, "No, no. That's not the way you ride a bike. You have to do it like this." You'd think that friend was crazy. The same goes for your baby. Refrain from giving instruction, let your baby discover how to move, and take delight as he practices each new position. You may notice that when your baby is first practicing a movement, walking, for instance, he will give his full attention to his balance and taking a step. When he has mastered a movement, he'll add to its complexity by manipulating an object at the same time he's moving. He'll hold an object, and once he can do so with ease, he may hold two objects, and eventually he may bang them together or swing them while taking steps. There's a lot to observe besides whether or not a baby or toddler is moving. If you observe closely, you'll notice *how* he's moving and what he's doing when he's in a particular position. Is he at ease as he takes those first tentative steps? Is he holding his breath or sticking out his tongue as he concentrates to find his balance before shifting his weight? Where is his focus as he moves? Is he looking at the object he's holding, at you, or at something else in the room? A lot of practice and learning takes place for your baby to progress from lying on his back to taking those first steps. By observing closely, you will be able to appreciate the practice and progress that is taking place. It's not as simple as "Is he sitting, standing, or walking?" because your baby is doing so much more than that.

HOW BABIES LEARN TO MOVE

As your baby moves, his brain receives feedback from his muscles and joints, and his developing nervous system gets important information about how his body functions so as to move harmoniously. When your young baby is placed on his back and allowed to move naturally, he will instinctively move in ways that will prepare him for the next stage in his developmental process. Rolling or lying on his tummy with his head raised will strengthen his spine and the core muscles that he will eventually need to comfortably and confidently maintain a sitting position.

Magda taught that a baby should never be put into a position that he can't get into on his own. When a baby is propped in a sitting position, for example, he is deprived of the opportunity to practice the essential skills that will prepare him for the next step of his gross motor development. His developmental sequence is interrupted. He may even skip important parts of the process that will inform his trunk muscles how to work together with ease. Stress will be put on his neck, trunk, and hips in a propped sitting position. His head may bob as he struggles to hold it upright, thus affecting his balance and vision. He may hold his breath. And what about the emotional impact? Your baby won't be able to relax if he's feeling gravity pulling him downward when he doesn't have the ability to maintain his balance on his own. He'll need to rely on a prop or on you to keep him upright. But what if you look away and he falls over? And even if you're vigilant, he'll still become startled when he *begins* to lose his balance, even if you catch him. If there's an interesting play object by his side, he may not be able to reach it without toppling over.

Many parents say, "But my baby *likes* to be propped into a sitting position so that he can see what's going on." A baby who has been routinely put into a sitting position will habituate to this position and protest when first laid on his back. He has learned to like the sitting position because it has become familiar to him—it's not because the sitting position provides a better view from which to see the activity going on around him. In fact, a baby who can't maintain a sitting position on his own can actually see far less than a baby on his back who can move his head to look all around and even behind him. Likewise, if no one has put a baby or toddler on a piece of crawling or climbing equipment and then hovered over him to keep him safe, he won't come to rely on someone else to ensure his safety. He will be inherently safer because he will have developed the habit of paying attention and relying on himself. He may approach a piece of equipment to investigate but will not crawl or climb onto it until he feels ready. And who better to know when he's ready than the baby himself? When he's ready to move, your baby will do so in a way that feels comfortable to him. He'll practice crawling up and down one step with confidence and ease before crawling up the second.

When your baby's gross motor development is allowed to

unfold naturally, he will acquire skills that go beyond finding balance, sitting up, and walking. As he discovers how to find balance in each new position, he'll learn to pay attention and to focus; he'll learn to problem-solve and to rely on himself to do so. When allowed to move in the way that is natural to him, without being coaxed or prodded to do more than he is capable of, he'll come to know that he's accepted just the way he is and that there's no pressure for him to move or to perform in a way that he's not yet ready for.

Cy has been later than many infants to develop certain motor skills, but thanks to RIE, we give him all the time he needs, allowing him to learn at his own pace. He is directing his own progress and is developing his own process, so not only do we get to watch him learn, but we are learning *how* he learns. And he is gaining the confidence that comes with each accomplishment. When he was first starting to roll over, he would roll onto one side and stay there for several minutes before rolling back. After a few weeks, he started rolling three-quarters of the way over and would settle into that position quite happily, never completing a full roll. A couple of months after other infants his age were rolling over, he eventually started rolling fully onto his belly. It was remarkable how graceful his movement was and how much pleasure he still experiences in the movement. He had fully enjoyed and prepared for every step of the process.

We did have to stop several well-intentioned friends and family members from "helping" him to roll over in the early stages, and we've had to check our own insecurities about comparing Cy to others. RIE helps us refocus on him and helps us resist the inclination to do too much for him at the expense of his own discoveries and adventures.

— Bianca Siegl

Every baby learns to move according to his own inner timetable. This may be of particular relevance for a child with developmental delays or challenges. Sometimes, well-intended parental assistance and interventions interfere with a child's ability to develop some of his *own* coping strategies. In her article about Molly, a child with special needs, Carol Pinto tells how the child, who could not yet crawl, taught herself how to roll down a ramp to get outside.[2] Molly's desire to be outdoors was a powerful motivator for her to figure out how to get outside on her own. Her caregiver could certainly have carried her outside, but doing so would have robbed Molly of the satisfaction that came from her own self-initiated movement. Magda taught us to notice and appreciate what a child *can* do rather than observing him from a deficit point of view.

One of the important takeaways from RIE is the idea of slowing down and allowing children to respond and develop according to their own individual timetables. Children who have developmental problems or challenges need that even more than other children. It doesn't mean that we don't offer them whatever therapy will help them cope with or overcome their challenges, but we must still have an attitude of trust in the child's own process. Parents who have a child with developmental challenges have suffered a blow to their faith in themselves as parents and to their sense that they can turn the child loose and everything will be fine. So they struggle. Maybe RIE can help them trust in a different kind of process.

— Ruth Anne Hammond, RIE Associate

New parent Jenny came to class, sat down, and placed her seven-month-old daughter, Ella, in front of her in a sitting position. All the other babies were still crawling and not able to push up to a sitting position on their own. Very quickly, one of the other babies, Mei, crawled over to investigate this new and unfamiliar baby and began to tug on her sleeve. Ella was stuck in the sitting position, unable to move. Her mother realized that this position was uncomfortable for her daughter not only physically but emotionally as well. She was unable to turn or move away from curious Mei, and she couldn't reach any of the play objects without risking tipping over. She wasn't able to be self-reliant because she needed her mother to keep her upright. It became clear to Jenny that propping her up certainly wasn't helping Ella develop a sense of competence and confidence. I encouraged Jenny to lay her daughter on her back, for just a few minutes initially, so that she could get used to this new position. Ella fussed at first because she'd gotten used to being in the upright position. But with the support of her mother, who sat close to her and sometimes even lay down next to her, Ella began to spend more and more time on her back until she was comfortable and content being there.

Lay your baby on his back on a flat and firm surface, so that he's free to move when and how he chooses. Every healthy baby will be most competent in this supine position, where his body is fully supported by the floor or surface beneath him. He can also fully relax in this position and will be able to move into another position when he chooses to do so.

Your newborn baby's movements will be jerky at first. His legs will be flexed or drawn up toward his abdomen, and his arms and hands may fly about suddenly. As the weeks go by, his movements will become smoother. He'll begin to practice rolling to one side and finding his balance there. He may do this for many weeks before he rolls over onto his tummy, either intentionally or to his surprise. When he first rolls onto his tummy, one of his arms may get stuck under his chest, and he will struggle to remove it. Helping him free his arm will not contribute to his learning how to accomplish this himself, so refrain from assisting and see what he can manage on his own. If he struggles for a while and then tires or becomes upset, you can turn him on his back or pick him up to comfort him. In time, he will learn how to get his arm out from under him with ease and efficiency.

After your baby becomes proficient rolling from back to tummy, he'll spend time stretching his arms out in front of him, reaching toward an object, and eventually crawling with his belly on the ground, toward the object. As he gains greater control of his body, horizontally first, then gradually coming to the vertical, he'll achieve gross motor milestones by practicing many incremental movements in between, until he's walking. He will learn to find balance and gain mastery in each new position before progressing to the next milestone.

At an RIE Parent-Infant Guidance class, fourteen-month-old Sam discovered a wooden box with an open side and a large hole on the top. He lowered himself into it, stood up with his head sticking out of the hole, and looked from one person to another with a big smile on his face. After banging a metal cup on the box for a minute, he was clearly puzzled about how to get out. He looked to his mom, Tracy, and she moved closer to him. She said, "You're trying to figure out how to get out of the box." He continued to try to solve his problem, periodically looking to his mom for reassurance. She said, "You pulled up your leg, but it doesn't fit through the hole." It might have been tempting for Tracy to lift him out of the box, but what would he have learned? With Tracy sitting on the floor nearby to offer emotional support, Sam was able to continue to problem-solve on his own and eventually figured out that by lowering his head and body, he could get out of the open side of the box. The grin on his face conveyed the satisfaction he felt at his own accomplishment. Sam discovered not only how to get out of the box but also that he could find a solution on his own. By refraining from rescuing Sam, Tracy discovered just how competent and capable he was on his own.

When an adult routinely steps in to solve every little, or big, problem, a baby can quickly learn to look for help rather than attempt to find a solution for himself, and giving up and relying on an adult for every little thing becomes a habit. Not only is the child robbed of a sense of self-satisfaction and accomplishment, but his sense of confidence and self-reliance can begin to erode as well. By allowing your baby's gross motor development to unfold naturally, you'll be supporting his physical and emotional development. Your baby will be able to relax because he'll never be put into a position that he's not able to get into on his own. Conversely, being "exercised" is not only uncomfortable but sends a message that "what you are able to do in this moment is not enough; I want you to do more." This can be a common occurrence for children with special needs, who, although they may need additional time to practice and perfect a particular movement, are often given much less.

Allowing your baby to develop according to his own schedule sends the message that you accept him where he is right now. You may have to restrain yourself from bursting into applause and cheering him on when he takes those first wobbly steps, but give him time. Learn to appreciate and take pleasure in how your baby is moving, in this moment. Let him be the one to decide if he wants to walk and how far. Observe how he's taking his first tentative steps rather than how far he's traveling. When he's ready to walk across the room, he will, and before you know it, he'll be running. Then you may look back and think, "What was the hurry?"

As I learned in my Parent-Infant Guidance class, a baby should never be put into a position that he can't get into on his own. Because I put this into practice when we went to the park, I never placed my boys on a climbing structure or monkey bars or helped them climb a tree. Because they were used to playing without interruption, they never asked me to help them. As they grew older, they could outclimb other children at the park, yet they weren't daredevils because they knew their own limitations.

My boys often watched other parents place their toddlers and even babies on the rings and in trees. William and Jackson waited a long time before they were able to get on the monkey bars and the hand-over-hand rings.

One day, while standing on the platform and looking at the rings, Jackson asked me, "Do you think it's safe?" I remember this moment distinctly because it was the only time that he asked *me* if he was able to do something.

I answered, "I don't know. Do you feel safe?" He looked at the bars and the ground below, thought about it, and then decided not to jump for the bars and climbed down.

When we went to the park the next day, I looked up and saw Jackson on the monkey bars, swinging from one to the next. He was so proud and felt such a sense of accomplishment. It had made that long wait worth every second. He conquered the monkey bars when he was ready to and on his own, using his own judgment and sense of safety.

I looked up at him and said calmly, "I see you're swinging on the bars." He did it for himself, not for me or anyone else.

— Jill Getto Lee, RIE Associate

CARRYING DEVICES AND EQUIPMENT

When considering equipment such as bouncers, walkers, slings, baby carriers, and backpacks, the question is "Whose need is being served?" Very often these devices serve the adult's need to hold a baby captive so that they can make dinner or take a shower. Of course, there are times when it's necessary for your baby to be in a car seat, carriage, or stroller, when you're traveling or doing errands. But none of these devices are ideal, because they inhibit your baby's free and natural movement. If your baby looks uncomfortable in a device, then he is. If you want to help your baby learn to self-soothe, there's no need to introduce a swing as a soothing device. If you have a safe area for play, there's no need for a bouncer whose primary purpose may be as a holding pen to keep your baby safe. Walkers don't help a new toddler learn to walk confidently and can actually be dangerous if the walker begins to move at a pace that the child can't keep up with. In addition, bouncers and swings put pressure on a baby's pelvic area and can cause the chest to compress. Babies are sometimes placed in backpacks before they're able to sit up on their own. They slump over and may hold on to the adult for balance. They may strain their backs and necks as they struggle to remain upright. When a baby is facing forward in a carrier, away from you, his legs are splayed, and his hips are open in an unnatural way. He can't turn his head to make eye contact with you, and seeing the world coming toward him, even at a slow pace, may cause him stress. If he's facing your chest, he has little ability to move his head, and no matter which way he's facing, he can't turn his head freely in response to a sound. Imagine you heard a noise that interested or startled you and were unable to turn your head to see what it was. While it may appear that a baby is relaxed when suspended in a carrier, being rendered immobile in this way can be a source of anxiety. A time when it *may* be advisable to use a carrier of some sort is when you need to walk with your baby as well as another child whose hand you must hold to keep safe.

Certainly, holding your baby and cuddling with him as you give him your full attention are important, but holding and cuddling are very different from "wearing" your baby in a device where the parent often pays little or no attention to the baby while doing something else. Magda suggested that it was preferable for your baby to spend some time in his crib or safe play area where he is free to stretch and move as he chooses. Then, when you are together, during caregiving or other times, you can give your baby your full and undivided attention.

What about strollers? For a baby who is not yet sitting up on his own, it's best for him to be flat on his back. There are "stroller systems" that allow your baby to be in the supine position during the early months. These strollers are ideal. Once your baby is sitting up, a rear-facing stroller is best. Britain's National Literacy Trust commissioned a study by Dundee University's School of Psychology to examine if there was any correlation between forward-facing strollers and language acquisition. Mothers apparently talked to their babies twice as much when their babies were in rear-facing strollers, where the two could make eye contact. This wasn't possible in forward-facing strollers, where the babies also showed higher degrees of stress. If you've navigated your way on a busy city sidewalk, just imagine being a young baby or toddler in a stroller, facing all that incoming traffic with your parent out of view behind you. If you decide to use a forward-facing stroller, be sure to take moments to connect with and reassure your child.

ENVIRONMENT, EQUIPMENT, AND CLOTHING

For your baby or toddler to have the freedom to move freely and independently, it's essential that he has a safe space in which to do it—one where he can move in whatever way he likes without risk of injury. If you take to heart the RIE principle of providing a safe play area, your baby will be free to move where and how he chooses, and you will be free to relax, knowing he's safe.

Some people believe that placing their babies on soft, cushioned surfaces will protect them from getting hurt, but a firm surface is best. It provides the stability your baby needs and feedback that will be informative as he works to find balance. Imagine trying to take your first steps on a squishy gym mat or shag rug versus an unyielding floor. Which would be easier? At RIE, we cover a foam play mat or braided rug with a cotton sheet, tucked in tightly underneath; this provides a smooth, clean surface for young babies who are not yet crawling. A wooden floor is best for crawling babies and toddlers who are beginning to walk because it's firm but also has some give to it. When babies begin to crawl, it's ideal to provide something safe for them to crawl onto and over. A heavy sofa cushion or bolster that's not too thick can serve the purpose quite well. When they start to pull up, they will need something stationary to pull up on. If your coffee table has round edges and is made of wood rather than glass, your baby may enjoy pulling up to standing while holding on to the table. Babies will certainly pull up on sofas, but a sofa is not safe to have in your baby's play area because your baby can eventually climb onto and fall off a sofa quite easily if you are not present.

For a baby to move freely, he needs clothing that won't restrict his movements. Those denim jeans may look adorable, but they're stiff, restrict the hips, bind the knees, and are difficult to crawl in. Overalls, dresses, and shorts that go over the knees can make crawling a challenge as well. Clothes that are made of soft materials and are formfitting—leggings, for example—allow a baby to move freely. In summer, your baby can wear nothing but a diaper.

Keep your baby's feet bare as often as possible. Observe your baby's feet and see how he articulates his toes. If he rolls over to his side, notice how he uses his toes—especially his big toe—for balance. If he's crawling, see how he uses them to push off so that he can move forward. Socks and shoes inhibit free movement, so let your baby do without them whenever you can. If your toddler is wearing shoes or sandals, the soles should be flexible. Avoid shoes that go above the ankle because they don't allow free movement of the ankle joint.

To practice moving, your baby needs space. How much space? For young babies who are not crawling, a small space is sufficient. At RIE, we have a five-foot round rug that we use for young baby classes that is ideal for one to four babies. Once your baby starts to roll or crawl, he'll need plenty of room to move in. An uncluttered, open space where he can move freely will benefit his gross motor exploration. Even in a very small apartment, try to find a corner where your baby can move freely. And, of course, the play space should be completely safe.

WHEN BABIES FALL

Finding balance requires losing balance from time to time. This is natural. No baby can learn to sit up, stand, and walk without sometimes losing his balance and falling. If we accept losing balance as a necessary part of the process, perhaps it can be easier to refrain from rushing in. When your baby falls, he may be startled or surprised; he may get a small bump or even a bloody lip. He may cry because he startled, rather than hurt, himself when he fell. Be available if he wants to be picked up, but don't assume this is what he wants. Instead it can help if you come close and narrate what you've seen. "You fell. That surprised you." Trust that he'll let you know if he wants you to pick him up or hold him. When we refrain from rescuing, babies learn that they need to pay attention, and we discover how resilient they can be. On the contrary, when we dive in to keep a baby from falling, he quickly learns to rely on someone else to catch him before he falls, and to ensure his safety. Ironically, this makes him *less* safe because he is not in the habit of focusing on how or where he is moving. This does not mean that we sit indifferently. We observe the baby and trust that he will let us know what he needs. We wait for his cue.

Once my daughter was walking, everywhere we went, someone would comment on how "careful" she was with herself—
how "competent" she was at moving, climbing, even falling.
People attributed it to her personality, but I know it was RIE. I
let her move, climb, and fall many times in a safe setting, and
so she always knew her physical limits and abilities.

—Aubrey Siegel

I once had a new baby come to class who had just begun to
stand up and take a step or two. I had placed a three-inch-high
rectangular platform for the babies to crawl onto. Some would
crawl up and over it; others would crawl onto it, pull up to standing, and then squat back down and crawl off. On his first day of
class, this baby crawled up onto the structure, stood up, looked at
me, stepped off the structure with his arms up in the air, and fell.
His mother said, "I think he thought you would catch him." A
baby who has learned to fall naturally, without being rescued,
will extend his arms forward when he falls. But this baby had
been practicing walking by holding on to an adult's hands and
therefore raised his hands in the air when he fell, as he was accustomed to doing. His mother later said that her baby had also
spent a lot of time jumping off his parents' bed into their waiting
arms. He had understandably assumed that someone would
always be there to catch him. In class, it quickly became clear to
the mother that her baby hadn't learned to pay attention to where
his body was on the floor or on a structure, and was therefore less
safe. She stopped the "catching baby" games at home and worked
with her son so that he could learn to pay attention and rely on
himself rather than others to keep him safe.

Babies in RIE Parent-Infant Guidance classes often approach a new piece of equipment with curiosity. They come close and frequently touch or tap it, but they don't just climb aboard. They explore it first and then interact with it in a way that feels comfortable. Babies who are allowed to develop according to their own physiological timetables develop an inner wisdom about what they can do and what they are not yet ready for.

One day in Parent-Infant Guidance class, Wyatt crawled up to the top of the small stair climber. He was enjoying lying on his tummy on the top, looking around at the parents and other babies, when all of a sudden he tumbled down and landed on his back at the bottom of the stairs. He began to wail, and his alarmed mother, Kristen, moved in quickly and began to pick him up. His response? He thrust his hand out in front of him, looked Kristen in the eyes, and grunted very loudly. There was no mistaking the meaning of that grunt. He did *not* want to be picked up. We all sat quietly while he cried, never moving from his back. As we observed Wyatt crying, we could see him processing what had happened and calming himself. After three minutes, his crying had lessened to a periodic whimper. Wyatt rolled onto his tummy, crawled over to his mother nearby, and pulled himself up onto her lap for a hug. I could see the relief on Kristen's face as she embraced him. Within a minute, refreshed and renewed, Wyatt crawled down from her lap, ready to explore the play area again. The group learned an important lesson about trusting the child to let you know what he needs.

What if your child is at the edge of a stair? Often an adult will say, "Be careful!" but those words are unspecific and of no use to the child. Be careful of what? Rather than preventing him from falling, your words may distract him, so that he *does* fall. If the circumstance is such that he will fall down one stair but be unharmed, the best course may be to let him fall, as this will be informative, and he will learn to pay closer attention the next time. If you're feeling anxious, you may want to go close, on his level, to ensure his safety, but do your best to be as unobtrusive as possible so that he can continue to focus on his balance. As usual, check in with yourself to see whether you're responding to your child's true need or to ease your own anxiety about a potential fall. It can take time and practice to pause and not rush in quickly.

Babies and toddlers love to move. They spend very little time in a static position, and when they do, it may be only for a fleeting moment. If you have any doubt that your baby is learning how to move—or even if you don't—get down on the floor and try to imitate his movements. Are you able to move as gracefully and fluidly as he does? You may be reminded of all the incremental movements that are necessary to roll onto your side or your belly or to come to a sitting position. You may find a deeper appreciation for everything your baby is doing and learning as he moves. It's breathtaking to see nature's plan unfold.

6. Play

Children play beautifully on their own. They do not need to be taught how to play.
—Magda Gerber and Allison Johnson, *Your Self-Confident Baby*

You don't have to teach your baby how to play. Instead babies can remind *us* how to play and have a sense of wonder about the world around us.

As Henry David Thoreau said, "What does education often do? It makes a straight ditch of a free, meandering brook." While Thoreau might have been talking about education, what does that have to do with young babies? A lot, I think. Many well-intentioned adults believe they need to begin teaching babies from birth. They count the rings as they pull them out of the box in front of a twelve-month-old child. They hold up a ball and ask the toddler what color it is. They pace the house with baby in arms, pointing at objects and naming them. But *teaching* a baby or toddler isn't necessary. When you trust that your baby will learn in the course of her everyday life, the time you spend with her will be a lot more pleasurable.

All babies are naturally curious and eager to engage with the world around them. At first they'll notice an interesting object and learn to grasp it so that they can bring it close to their mouths to explore orally. Like scientists, they manipulate objects in a variety of ways, and in ways that are meaningful to *them*. We certainly can't know what is intriguing to a baby at any particular moment, so it's important for the baby to follow her own curiosities and see where they take her. Imagine that you're curious about a camera and thoroughly absorbed in trying to understand how it works. How would you feel if someone interrupted you to say something unimportant or unrelated or began to give you a lesson on the camera's lenses? Do you suppose you'd want to stop your exploration to listen to the tutorial, or do you think you'd prefer to carry on making your own discoveries? To be present during uninterrupted play, it's necessary for us to step back a little, to be "less important," and to follow the baby's lead.

If your baby isn't hungry or tired, if it's not time for a new diaper or a bath, and if she is emotionally ready for play, then she can be laid down in her play area. Then it's up to her to decide *if* she wants to play. Perhaps your young baby would prefer to lie on her back and gaze up at the light overhead for a while. It's your baby's decision *when* to play. You may feel impatient, wishing she would reach over for that lovely new play object, but try to let go of that thought and just see what happens.

WHY UNINTERRUPTED PLAY IS IMPORTANT

Babies, even the youngest infants, need time for uninterrupted play every day. By uninterrupted, we mean just that. Let your baby choose what object to play with, how to play with it, and for how long. Refrain from giving an object to your baby and showing her how to do something "fun" with it or how it should be used. Let your baby be the author of her play. Sit quietly on the floor nearby, on your hands if you must, and simply observe and take pleasure in what your baby is doing. What object does she seem to be interested in? How does she grasp it: with her left hand or her right? Does she use all her fingers to take hold of the object or just her thumb and index finger? Does she put the object in her mouth or tap it on the floor or against another object? Is she moving her feet as she plays? Perhaps she's lying on her side, using the big toe of one of her feet to balance. For toddlers, how are they using the objects? Are they collecting or dumping? Do you see the beginnings of dramatic play?

Babies learn many important things through play:

- **Cause and effect.** When they bang an object on the floor, it makes a noise. Two different objects, of different materials, make different noises.

- **Problem solving.** When they turn a jar lid back and forth, it doesn't come off, but when they turn it in just one direction, and keep on turning, it *does* come off.

- **Trial and error.** Like scientists, they learn about the different properties of objects. The ball will roll down the ramp, but the teddy bear won't. Similar-looking objects can have different weights and textures.

Your baby also learns what her preferences are and what interests her. If an adult refrains from swooping in to solve every little problem, your baby will learn to accept challenge and struggle as a necessary part of life and learning. As Magda said, "There is dignity in struggle. It gives our soul muscle." Your baby can learn to try and try again and not to give up easily.

Play is about discovery and gives babies the opportunity to learn about the people and the environment around them. Play can support the development of self-confidence, self-reliance, focus and attention, and, with practice, fine motor and gross motor skills. Magda taught that play should be open-ended and simply for play's sake. Young babies have no particular goal in mind when they're manipulating a play object. In fact, having a goal is an adult point of view, so let your baby experiment and discover freely.

When adults look at a bowl of plastic pop beads, for example, our first instinct is usually to pop them together. But when we set up for an RIE Parent-Infant Guidance class, the beads are presented unattached to one another in a colander or other container. By setting them out that way, we don't imply they should be put together. Young babies and toddlers use the beads in a variety of ways by grasping them, chewing on the nib end, putting their fingers in the holes, and using them as screwdrivers to "fix" things in the room. Toddlers like to collect them in a bucket and dump them out. I've never seen a baby or toddler (remember, they're under two!) put the beads together. But I have seen parents, quite unconsciously, put the beads together if some happen to be nearby. What happens next? A child notices the string of beads, takes them apart, can't get them back together on her own, and gestures for her parent to do it for her. Cognitively, she may not be ready to figure out how the beads pop together, and she may not have the fine motor skills to accomplish the task. Because she isn't able to put the beads together on her own, the parent's doing so leads to frustration that could easily have been avoided.

At first it was difficult for me not to "rescue" my twin boys while they were playing. I guess I viewed babies as helpless. I remember literally sitting on my hands while watching them during uninterrupted play. That gave me a couple of seconds before responding, which was just enough time for me to stop myself from interfering. When I waited to see what would happen and didn't intervene, I was surprised to learn how competent my boys were. They were capable of resolving their own conflicts and solving many of their own problems. This is where the seed of trust in their competency began.

— Jill Getto Lee, RIE Associate

A SPACE FOR PLAY

Remember Magda's definition of a safe play space? It's one where if your baby was left on her own all day, she would be hungry, upset, and need a new diaper when you returned, but she would be physically unharmed. When I ask parents if they have a safe space at home for their baby, they often say, "It's *almost* completely safe." Maybe everything is safe except that one standing lamp in the corner of the room that the baby could pull over. If so, then the environment is *not* safe. You may want to ask someone else to look at the safe space you've created because they may notice trouble spots that you have not seen. I encourage you to do whatever is necessary to create a safe space in your home. If you have to be on the alert to ensure your baby's safety, or if you have to strap her into a device so that she's captive while you go to the bathroom, then you can't fully implement the Educaring Approach. Some parents are reluctant to put up gates or to sacrifice space to provide a safe area for their babies, but when they do, the common refrain is that life becomes so much easier, and they can finally relax.

We put our dining table and chairs in storage and set up a gated area off the kitchen that is completely safe. This made a huge difference in our ability to allow our son to play on his own without our having to continually intervene to make sure he was safe. It freed me up to be able to go to the bathroom or take a quick shower if need be. He can play in that area, and I know he is totally safe.

— Natascha Corrigan Aldridge

Until your baby is a few months old, most of her waking time will be spent being fed, diapered, and bathed. What little awake time remains can be spent in her crib or playpen; it's okay if this is the same space she sleeps in. Since a larger space can be overwhelming to a very young baby, her crib or playpen is ideal. Here she can feel cozy and secure in a confined space, as opposed to lying on a blanket on the floor of an open room. When your baby is a little older and you see that she's ready, she can lie on her back on a mat or rug covered with a plain cotton bedsheet, tucked in around the sides. The sheet can be washed and changed whenever necessary. You can choose to dispense with the sheet whenever you like, of course, but at RIE we generally wait until the babies are all sitting up. By making the play area a "no outdoor shoes area," you can ensure that the floor is clean, particularly for young babies, who may mouth or lick the floor.

We made Cy's bedroom a safe play space. It has made an enormous difference for all of us! We are able to leave the room to do household tasks with the confidence that he will continue to play without risk of injury.

Many of the lists of developmental milestones for six- to eight-month-olds state that infants should know and respond appropriately to the word *no* at this age. Because Cy is free to play safely in his room, and RIE has given us the tools to communicate effectively with him, we hardly ever say no to him. It is not that we don't and won't have limits, of course, but having a safe play space means that we don't have an occasion to tell him no. Corrections of his behavior come more in the form of explaining how to be gentle when touching our faces or petting our family cat than in any version of a sharp "no!"

— Joanna Hankamer

It's ideal for your baby to have an indoor and an outdoor space for play and wonderful if the outdoor space is accessible to the baby. In Parent-Infant Guidance classes at the Los Angeles RIE Center, doors from the indoor classroom open onto a shaded deck, so that crawling babies can go in and out as they choose. Of course, this is not possible in most homes, but do think about spending some time outdoors each day. People frequently assume that the place for gross motor play (climbing, walking, running, etc.) is outdoors, and indoors should be reserved for more quiet activity, but ideally the outdoors should provide opportunities for quiet activity as well.

In their book *The Elephant in the Living Room*, pediatrician Dimitri Christakis and public health advocate Frederick Zimmerman write about the "habits of mind." They state that "the ability to stay focused is not entirely determined by a person's brain structure or genes. Interactions with the environment can also play a role in *teaching* focus."[1] In other words, babies who live in a home that is peaceful are given the opportunity to *develop* focus, as opposed to those who live in a home where the television supplies the sound track and the parent frequently jumps up to answer the phone or respond to the beep of a text or e-mail. The American Academy of Pediatrics discourages any kind of media use for children under two years.[2] If you have a safe environment for your baby to play in, you won't have to resort to the television as a babysitting device. The AAP also discourages secondhand television exposure where the adult is watching a program or the television is on in the background. Because babies aren't born with the ability to filter out unwanted stimuli, they pay attention to everything, and a busy, noisy environment does not provide the opportunity for babies to focus their attention. In this fast-paced world, where many of us are bombarded by input, it is increasingly important to have the ability to tune out unnecessary chatter to focus on what is important.

How Much Space?

Young babies who are not rolling onto their sides yet can be content in a crib or playpen. Once they are moving, babies need more—but not too much—space to move about in and practice their emerging gross motor skills. Dr. Pikler noted that "infants move about and play less in unlimited than in clearly defined spaces."[3]

A friend of mine whose son was crawling called me in exasperation. Annie said, "Everywhere I move, Joey is right at my heels. I'm afraid I'm going to step on him! He has the run of the whole house, so why is he always underfoot?" Joey needed to stay close to his mom because the entire house was overwhelming to him. He just didn't feel secure having so much space. I suggested to Annie that she put up gates to create a much smaller, defined space for Joey, which she did. Annie put some play objects in the area and spent time there with Joey, "endearing" the space to him. Although gates may seem prisonlike to adults, for babies, gates provide limits and a sense of security. It's ideal to put up gates before your baby starts to move because then the gates will just be part of her familiar environment. Conversely, when a baby starts moving and a gate suddenly appears, she will naturally protest this new limitation to her freedom of movement.

WHEN TO INTRODUCE PLAY OBJECTS

You may notice that your newborn has quite a grip. She may clench her fists, which will sometimes find their way to her mouth. If you place something in her hand—your finger, perhaps—she will hold on tightly. In fact, research has shown that your newborn baby's "grasp reflex" can actually have a calming affect, causing her heart rate to decelerate as she grasps your finger.[4] Until she's some weeks older, she won't be able to intentionally release something placed in her hand. Eventually this reflex will fall away, and she'll be able to grasp an object and let it go when she chooses. Her hand and arm movements will become purposeful, so that she can move toward and grasp an object that interests her.

Babies don't need play objects during the first weeks of life. Nearly all their waking time will be spent being fed, diapered and bathed, and adapting to their environment. Eventually your baby will remain awake for longer periods, during which she can simply lie on her back in her crib or playpen or on a blanket on the floor. From there she can turn her attention to herself or take in the environment around her. Sometime around three months of age, you'll notice your baby discovering her hands. Lying on her back, she'll raise her hands in front of her face. At first it will seem that she's not aware that the hands actually belong to her; she'll have little control of them as they move about in front of her. Over time, she'll gain control of her hands and will move them consciously, grasping one hand in the other. When you observe this, it's a good time to introduce just a few (three or four) play objects. A parent's first instinct may be to hand a toy to a baby and suggest that she play with it, but handing an object to a baby implies that it's time to play. Maybe she's enjoying lying quietly, just gazing at the tree out the window. Remember that your baby has a point of view and preferences, so let her decide when to play, what object to play with, and what she'd like to do with it.

The biggest immediate benefit of starting RIE with our baby was recognizing just how overstimulating everything could be. She didn't need (or want, truly) toys hanging in her face or music or lights in a play gym, in the car seat, or in her crib! She could lie on her back and look at her hands for an hour, very happily. Feeling confident about turning the "volume" of everything down helped our whole family.

— Aubrey Siegel

PLAY OBJECTS

Babies don't need complicated, expensive toys to play with. They demonstrate this whenever they toss aside the carefully considered present for the tissue paper and gift box. Toy manufacturers would have us believe that children need toys to stimulate their senses and to entertain and teach them. But these are certainly not necessary, and over and over again, babies tell us so. When parents listen, they can save huge sums on unnecessary toys and have the pleasure of living in a home with far less clutter.

The dictionary defines a toy as "something meant to be played with, especially by children." But a play object is *anything* that your baby chooses to manipulate that is safe for her to engage with. How do you determine if an object is safe? First of all, it has to be made of a material that is safe for your baby to mouth, lick, and chew on. If it can fall through a toilet paper roll, it's too small and is a choking hazard. If a baby can get an entire object in her mouth, then it's too small and is unsafe. Educaring objects are *passive*. In other words, they don't do a thing until the *active* baby manipulates them. They don't move, unless the baby causes them to move. They don't light up. They don't make sounds, unless the baby hits the play object on the floor or against another object. The rule of thumb is passive play object, active child.

The Educaring environment supports a baby to actively participate in her play by being an explorer and a scientist, discovering the different properties of various objects and what happens when she manipulates them. Conversely, when a baby has toys that "entertain," she quickly learns that during playtime, she can simply do nothing and be entertained. It's easy to see how the thoughtful selection of play objects can have implications for your baby that go far beyond baby and toddlerhood.

Baby's first play objects should be soft, so that a young baby who is unable to release her grip will not hurt herself with a hard object. Dr. Pikler recommended using a plain cotton napkin, and this is what we do at RIE. (Napkins made of silk or synthetics or that have tassels or other decorative elements are unsafe and should not be used.) When setting up the environment, lay the napkin out flat on the play mat, grasp it in the center, and pull up so that it forms a peak. When your baby becomes interested in the napkin, watch how she studies and investigates it. She may wave, mouth, and crush it. A simple cloth can consume her focus and attention. It's lightweight and breathable, so it can't hurt if it touches her face. Don't be alarmed if your baby grasps the napkin, brings it overhead, and releases it on top of her nose and mouth. She'll be able to turn her head and breathe and will learn to whisk it away from her face.

To the napkin, we might add a small cotton, silicone, or rubber play object, something that can easily be grasped and cannot hurt her if she inadvertently bangs it against her head. Your baby can enjoy playing with the same objects for weeks or months, getting to know them and explore them in a variety of ways. She does not need an ever-changing or large variety of play objects to keep her interest. Place the objects near your baby but not right next to her, so that she can see and reach for them. Another object can be a little farther away, requiring more of an effort to reach.

What about rattles? We don't recommend them because usually the baby can't see what is making the noise, and if she can, she can't touch the noisemaking part of the rattle. Remember cause and effect? We want the baby to understand what's making the noise and why. When she bangs a metal cup against the floor and it makes a sound, she learns about cause and effect. With a rattle, she can't see or touch the noisemaking part of the object. Let the baby be the one to "make the noise," by banging an object against something. She may then bang two objects against each other and discover that they make a different sound than when she bangs just one of them on the floor. Aha! She's made a discovery.

What other objects *do* we find in an Educaring environment? Many can be found in the home or have other uses: plastic hair rollers, metal frozen-juice lids and canning rings, colanders, silicone pot holders and muffin cups, plastic nesting cups or boxes, wood or metal napkin rings (unpainted), wood butter molds, small metal cups, empty plastic water or laundry detergent bottles (without the cap and thoroughly washed), balls (Wiffle or others that are bumpy or smooth, made of cotton, plastic, or rubber), and other similar objects. It's not necessary to provide gender-specific toys for young babies and toddlers. In other words, boys and girls can enjoy playing with the same objects, whether they're balls, trucks, or dolls. For toddlers, have plenty of balls and things that roll, like cars and trucks. Toddlers like to collect, so have objects to carry things in, like bowls and buckets. When toddlers begin dramatic play, dolls, doll blankets, hats, and purses can be added. Older toddlers may enjoy "cleaning up" with a little whisk broom and dustpan.

When you're preparing the environment, lay out the play objects in such a way that you don't suggest how they should be played with. This means leaving the pop beads unattached and the nesting cups apart. You know those children's bowling sets? Set one or two pins out lying down and let your child discover that the pins can be stood up and knocked down. I've never seen a toddler under two actually stand a pin upright, but I've often seen the bowling pin used as a percussion instrument or a croquet mallet to hit a ball.

Small objects, referred to as *manipulatives*, provide opportunities for babies to grasp or *manipulate* the object and develop fine motor skills. These may be plastic links, rings or keys, or small wooden cups. For a young baby who has just started or may not yet be rolling over, we might set out a tented cotton napkin, metal juice lid, silicone muffin cup, and wood ring for her to mouth and grasp. For crawling babies, a few more objects would be added, with a variety of textures and densities. We might include several small cups of wood, metal, and plastic; a colander with plastic hair curlers or rings; and a doll and stuffed animal.

For toddlers, notice what they're doing with the objects. If the toddler is collecting, include some empty buckets, baskets, and bowls in the play area. If she is sorting, add manipulative objects that can be sorted by shape, type, or color. Include a doll for imaginative play and bring out the cloth napkins, which will perhaps now be used as doll blankets. Set out the objects in an orderly fashion so that your child knows, for instance, that the balls always start the day in that corner, the dolls in a basket under the window, the rings in the colander by the door, and so on. As RIE Associate Beverly Kovach once said, "Imagine how you'd feel if you went to make your morning coffee and someone had rearranged your kitchen in the middle of the night." Setting up the play area in the same predictable way every day will provide a sense of security for your child and support her ability to develop mastery of the space. As your child grows, you can introduce additional objects that may provide more complex challenges: nesting cups and plastic jars with lids, for example. When we observe that a child has been uninterested in a certain object for a few days, we may "retire" it for a while and bring it out sometime later to see if there is renewed interest. Remember too that less is more. Don't clutter the space with a lot of objects. Start with just a few objects and observe how your baby interacts with them.

In RIE Parent-Infant Guidance classes, as the babies develop and are able to move around the play area, we add a few more play objects to the environment. There are many objects that the children play with for twenty months and more. As a child's fine and gross motor skills develop, she will manipulate and use the objects in new and more complex ways.

Play Objects That RIE Children Enjoy

For precrawling babies:

Frozen-juice lids and canning rings (metal)

Hair curlers (plastic)

Manipulatives: links, rings, keys, pop beads, small cups or saucers (plastic, metal, or wood)

Muffin cups and small pot holders (silicone)

Napkins (plain cotton, tented)

For crawling babies, add a few of these:

Balls of various sizes, textures, and colors, of cloth or rubber. (We don't introduce balls until the baby is crawling. For a nonmobile baby, it can be frustrating to touch a ball and have it roll away, out of reach.)

Bottles: water or laundry detergent (without caps, thoroughly cleaned)

Bowling pins: child size (lying down)

Bowls (metal and plastic) and colanders (plastic)

Butter molds (wooden)

Containers or other holders of various shapes and sizes (plastic or fabric)

Cups (plastic, wooden, or metal)

Dolls with clothes that snap or zip, to practice taking on and off when she's a toddler (cloth or vinyl)

Stacking or nesting cups or boxes (plastic or metal)

Stuffed animals (just a few)

For toddlers, add a few of these (but don't overwhelm your child with too many play objects):

Things to roll: cars, trucks

Containers to collect things in: buckets, bowls, and purses (fabric, wooden, woven, or plastic)

Jars or other containers with lids that lift off or lids that unscrew (plastic, metal, or woven)

Puzzles

Hats and purses

THE PARENT'S ROLE DURING PLAY

If you don't have to teach your baby how to play and you don't have to be her playmate, then what *is* your role during your baby's playtime? As always, the adult is responsible for providing an environment that is calm and peaceful, with developmentally appropriate objects and equipment for gross motor exploration. There may be wants nothing times when you can enjoy being with your baby as she plays in her safe play area. Sit nearby, on the floor is best, so that your baby can see you and move toward you when she chooses. Your baby may crawl away from you to investigate something on the other side of her play space. You may notice her looking over her shoulder to check in with you. Your attention, emotional availability, and peaceful enjoyment will support her to venture out to explore the environment, knowing you'll be there to return to for emotional refueling when she needs it.

Babies can be easily distracted, so you may notice how little it takes to interrupt your baby's play. Even shifting your weight slightly can be enough to cause your baby to turn her attention from her play to you, so do your best to be a peaceful presence. Of course, there will be times when you need to interrupt her play, so do as you would with an adult and apologize for interrupting. There will be other times that you won't want to be or can't be with your baby as she plays. Perhaps you need to get some work done, make a phone call, or prepare a meal. Not only can your baby learn to play peacefully on her own, but she may actually enjoy spending quiet time alone for a while. Of course, all babies have their own unique temperaments, and some babies will want you nearby more than others. But it is a revelation to many parents that leaving their baby to play in a safe play space is not deprivation or an act of abandonment but can actually be pleasurable for the baby as she explores and experiments freely, without interruption.

Providing time for uninterrupted play does not mean that you must always be quiet and subdued with your baby. As a matter of fact, it is important to share moments of high affect, or "joy states," with your baby, not only during playtime but at other times throughout the day as well. As RIE Associate Ruth Anne Hammond points out in *The RIE Manual*, "The importance of the adult in helping the child achieve joy states...is something all good and loving parents intuitively do, through various playful interactions."[5] Your baby may squeal with delight as you "blow raspberries," and kick her legs in anticipation of the next funny sound you make. As Hammond adds, "Being sensitive to the baby's capacity to handle high and low arousal, the sensitive adult leads (and follows) the baby up and down in excitement, based on intuitively felt feedback between adult and infant. We may not notice when it is happening smoothly, but when the adult is overstimulating or understimulating, the mismatch is more evident."[6] Take pleasure in joyful interactions with your baby while doing your best to pay attention to her cues. Maintaining balance is key so that pleasurable joy states don't lead your baby to become overstimulated. When this happens, she may need you to help her to calm, or she may stop squealing or look away from you to disengage, thus sending a clear signal that she's done.

Some parents believe the optimum way of achieving joy states is to tickle their babies, throw them into the air and catch them, or hang them upside down. Some older toddlers may seek out and enjoy this kind of roughhousing, but it is not a respectful way to play with a baby. It is not initiated by the baby and treats her as little more than an object. Perhaps a baby's hysterical laughter in response to these kinds of interactions is confusing, leading the adult to believe that laughter equals delight. But laughter does not always convey pleasure and may instead be an expression of fear and anxiety. If we observed more closely, we might notice a baby tense her limbs, widen her eyes, and purse her lips when being thrown in the air—in this case, all manifestations of her anxiety.

As your baby grows, she may extend her hand to show you a play object—don't mistake it as a gift, because it's probably not. A toddler who is involved in dramatic play may offer you a mud pie or a "cup of tea." This can be fun, and without thinking, you might launch into a monologue about how the tea is delicious and, in so doing, change the course of the play. Instead, do as little as possible and follow your child's lead. Try not to make assumptions about her script or idea. It can be delightful to take part in this way—letting your child be the author and director, with you acting as a mere supporting player. But when an adult gets carried away in the play, he or she can quickly and unintentionally hijack it.

At class, a toddler who was new to the RIE group brought a small silicone pot holder to her mother, who held it up in front of her face and said, "Hot! Hot!" The child looked quizzically at her mother, not understanding why on earth her mother was saying "Hot!" This object was merely something she'd enjoyed shaking about and using as a saucer for muffin cups. She had no idea what a pot holder was, and the "Hot! Hot!" comment just did not compute. Her mother realized how she might have said something like "I see. You're holding the pot holder," leave it at that, and see what her daughter had in mind next. It's interesting to observe how our participation affects a child's play.

I remember feeling such relief after learning that I didn't have to act particularly silly, musical, or adventurous to connect to my son. I simply needed to tune out all other distractions and be present. It took a lot of pressure off of finding the right toys or planning the right excursion, but it also demanded a lot of self-control to put away my smartphone and put off household chores to give him all my attention.

—Chet Callahan

Observing Your Baby at Play

Observing your baby during uninterrupted play may be challenging at first. It may be hard to sit still without talking or commenting. It may be all you can do not to touch your baby or hand a play object to her. Just remember that you'll have plenty of time to cuddle later! You may realize that you're leaning over your baby rather than sitting back in a relaxed and comfortable position. Your mind may wander, and you may find yourself daydreaming or composing an e-mail in your head. It can take time to learn to observe your baby as she plays, so practice by observing for just five minutes to begin with. See if you can be fully present and quiet at the same time. Be available to your baby if she looks to you or needs you, but try not to be intrusive. Honor her separateness, as strange as that may sound. So many parents have told me that observation was difficult at first but soon became a particularly precious time with their baby.

In Parent-Infant Guidance class, parents often bring questions from home, but the curriculum is largely emergent. This means that we talk about what's actually happening in class that day. Since we're there to observe, in order to understand the babies and their behavior, it's necessary to have some discussion about how we see the babies engaging with objects and each other. We do this as respectfully as we can and speak generally about the children rather than using their names. If a child is paying attention to the conversation, we'll acknowledge it. We might say, "We're talking about when you and Jessie were on the steps." We show respect by not talking about a child in front of her as if she didn't understand.

One of the things that I have noticed in my work with parents and toddlers through the years is how RIE parents have learned to observe and stay steady while their child struggles for mastery. They are willing to let the child experience the joy and delight of mastery. This seems to foster confidence and resilience. I also personally love the full attention given to caring interactions such as diapering and feeding. It is truly a pleasure to work with these families.

— Carol Provost, nursery school teacher

GENUINE ACKNOWLEDGMENT

Magda taught us to reflect what we see instead of praising. "You got those rings apart." "You put the nesting cups together." Acknowledge and share in your child's pleasure of her accomplishment. "You got the lid off. You look really happy about that." Refrain from adding an evaluative judgment, which does nothing to build self-esteem but, in fact, most often has the opposite effect. As the educator Alfie Kohn says in his article "Five Reasons to Stop Saying Good Job," " 'Good job!' doesn't reassure children; ultimately, it makes them feel less secure. It may even create a vicious circle such that the more we slather on the praise, the more kids seem to need it, so we praise them some more. Sadly, some of these kids will grow into adults who continue to need someone else to pat them on the head and tell them whether what they did was OK. Surely this is not what we want for our daughters and sons."[7]

When we use words that acknowledge a child's efforts, we

send the message that the acquisition of skills is a process that happens over time. "You're working hard to unzip your sweatshirt." "You were really pumping your legs on the swing." Conversely, when we make statements like "Good job," we are speaking about the end result and not the effort it took to get there. Even worse, "You're so smart" sends the message that the child has achieved something just because of her intelligence—not through her efforts. But what happens to this child when she's faced with a challenging task? She may give up, saying, "I can't!" She has come to see her intelligence and ability as predetermined and fixed, that she can either do something easily or not. If an adult hasn't correlated her intelligence to her achievements, when presented with a challenge, the child will likely think, "This is hard. I guess I'll have to keep at it to figure it out." She will understand and accept that challenge and failure are both part of the process.

Magda's Criteria for Praise

Do not praise a child who is happily playing.
Do not praise a child who is "performing" for adults.
Praise a child for social adaption—for doing things that are very difficult, like waiting or sharing.[8]

WHAT *IS* SHE DOING?

What is she doing when she's manipulating play objects and moving them around? Your baby's playtime is not just idle time. Important discoveries are being made, and significant learning is taking place. Your baby is learning about the properties of various objects, to be sure. But she's also practicing and acquiring fine and gross motor skills. Through repetition and practice, she's learning how to learn. When given plenty of time for uninterrupted play, she's developing the ability to focus and to have a long attention span. She's learning to tolerate struggle to problem-solve, and that challenge is a necessary part of life. If your baby is able to roll over to her tummy but not yet able to crawl, she may reach and reach for an object that may remain just beyond her fingertips. You may feel uncomfortable and impatient as you watch her stretch to reach that ring. It may be all you can do not to pick up the ring and hand it to her. But wait! When you don't swoop in to rescue your baby at every little struggle, she'll discover her own inner reserves and tenacity. She'll follow her own curiosities to whatever interests and pleases *her*, rather than what may interest and please *you*. By sitting back and observing your baby at play, you'll be able to see her more clearly, in all her uniqueness. If you've made a habit of not rescuing her, you will discover that what you assumed would frustrate her, in fact, does not. When she reaches for the ring, she'll be able to tolerate not being able to quite get to it. She may look around for another object to pursue. She may enjoy just *looking* at the objects and space around her. Or she may make the ingenious discovery that I've seen some babies make, which is to get hold of the sheet and pull it up, thus causing the object to slide toward her! Those young scientists would never have made these discoveries if their parents had done the problem solving for them.

Educaring has made parenting so much easier. There are so many messages thrown at parents about how to stimulate your baby and help him to develop — so many things to *do* — that it is both a relief and an incredible boost of confidence to just *be*. We are able to slow down and appreciate our son, observe his developing abilities, and simply enjoy our time together. Being able to toss out agendas and trust our son is a remarkable gift for all of us.

— Bianca Siegl

ALLOW YOUR TODDLER TO PROBLEM-SOLVE

A young toddler is struggling to undress a doll. She pulls and pulls on the snaps of the doll's Onesie, but to no avail, and becomes increasingly frustrated. She goes to her mother and thrusts the doll into her hands, gesturing for her to remove the doll's outfit, which the mother promptly does. Mother does this, of course, because she quite naturally wants to help her daughter. But does this "help" give her daughter any information she can use next time she wants to undress the doll? Unfortunately, no. The mother's response of unsnapping the snaps may be efficient, but it robs her child of the opportunity to practice and master this fine motor skill. It also sends a message to the child that she can't do it on her own. Instead the mother can acknowledge her daughter's challenge by saying, "It's hard to unsnap the snaps." Knowing that her mother has observed her difficulty and is paying attention may provide all the support the child needs to persevere. If it doesn't, the child may ask for her mother's help. Then her mother might say,

"Let's do this together. First, let's unsnap the snaps," as she places her hands near the top snap so that her daughter can place her hands there, too. They can pull the snap open together, so that her daughter can feel the sensation of pulling the snap open. They may have to do this many times before the child learns to do it on her own. In this way, the mother offers support, in such a way that she assists her daughter's learning and growing independence at the child's own pace.

There may be times when a child's refrain of "I can't" means "I'm tired" or "I want to do this with you, not by myself." In these instances, giving your attention and offering emotional support may be all that is needed. Saying, "I know you can do it" or "You don't need my help," disregards the child's point of view and can feel like a lack of interest. You are telling the child to figure it out on her own when she has made it clear that she needs you. If your child says, "I can't," the simplest thing may be to stop what you're doing, get down on the floor with her, and ask what she needs. If she's tired or overly frustrated, she may opt for a warm hug from you instead.

PUTTING OBJECTS AND PLAYTHINGS AWAY

At the end of RIE classes, it's time to put away the play objects. Just as we move slowly during caregiving routines to allow the baby to understand the process and participate if she chooses, we move slowly as we put away the play objects. With young babies who are not yet rolling over, I bring out the big blue bowl that we use just for collecting play objects at the end of class. I slowly pick up the objects, one by one, and put them into the bowl, narrating here and there. "Now I'm putting the napkin in the bowl." "Here's a lid." "The doll is going into the bowl." Because I move *very* slowly, the young babies are able to follow each object with their eyes as it moves from floor to bowl. By the time babies are crawling, they may pick an object up and drop it into the bowl themselves. Babies and toddlers can enjoy participating in what to an adult is a mundane task. If they want to participate, they'll drop the objects in the bowl; if they don't want to, I take my time to complete the job myself. I ask the parents to sit quietly and observe so that the children can focus on the process. If six or more adults suddenly stood and started tossing things into the bowl, the children would be focusing not on the task but on the sea of legs that had suddenly appeared above them. We can't expect a baby or toddler to put away his toys, but modeling the process is a good place to start. You can narrate how you're putting the balls into the basket and the cups on the shelf. When play objects always return to their own particular place at the end of each day, it helps the child to develop a sense of order.

READING TO BABIES

Reading books can be a delightful experience to share with your baby and can support your baby's language development as well. As long as your baby is still using her mouth to explore objects, I recommend that the books *not* be readily available to her, unless they're made of cloth or wood. It's unrealistic to ask a child who is mouthing and biting objects not to do the same to a book. You can keep books on a shelf and bring them down to look at together. Take your cue from your baby as to when she's ready to go to the next page. She may want to linger on that picture of the rooster for quite a while. She may want to start in the middle of the book and then turn to the page before. Remember that even the notion of reading a book from cover to cover is an adult point of view, so if all your child wants to do is ponder one page for several minutes, that's fine. Reading can be a lovely part of the ritual before going to sleep at night.

WHEN BABIES PLAY TOGETHER

Magda taught about the importance of small group size. At RIE, we don't have more than six or seven babies together in a class, and we know that most often, at least one baby will not be present because she is sick or napping. Groups any larger can be overstimulating for babies, particularly when they are young. In Parent-Infant Guidance classes, the groups are organized not by age but according to how the babies are moving, so that we don't have a toddler in the same group as babies who are not yet rolling to their sides. At first, the babies will lie side by side and may gaze at one another with curious interest. They may reach out a hand to touch another baby. When they begin to roll over and crawl, they may intentionally move closer to another baby to explore. At these times, many well-meaning adults separate the babies, but at RIE we believe that as long as an attentive adult is nearby to offer support and intervene when necessary, these interactions can be valuable learning opportunities for the babies.

Do your best to sit back and let the babies explore one another freely; don't hover. Intervene only when an issue of safety arises. Babies can be fascinated with one another, so it's only natural for them to move closer to find out what this other person is all about. Young babies explore objects by touching and mouthing them, so don't be alarmed when your baby interacts with another baby by touching and mouthing her as well. If neither baby has teeth, mouthing can be a safe way to explore. If one or both of the babies *do* have teeth and one baby is about to put her mouth on another, move in and put your hand between one baby's mouth and the other's cheek to prevent contact. You might say, "I won't let you bite David. Here's something you *can* bite," and offer two play objects to choose from.

Hair can be enticing, and a young baby, who may not be able to release her grip, can get quite a hold of another baby's hair—or yours. If this happens, softly rub the top of your baby's hand; this will likely cause her hand to open. If it doesn't, gently remove her hand from the other baby's hair. As you do this, you might say something like, "Gentle. That hurts Sylvie when you pull her hair." Gently stroke one baby's head and then the other's. In this way, both babies can feel what it's like to be touched gently and will come to learn the meaning of the word.

Don't be alarmed if your young baby tries to explore another baby by swatting or poking. This is a natural way for a young baby to explore and doesn't imply that your child is aggressive or unkind.

Toddlers may push or hit. They may do so out of frustration or anger, or just to discover how others will respond. They may act aggressively because they are tired, hungry, or over-stimulated, or because they need an adult to consistently provide limits until they've internalized the limits and can successfully manage their impulses. When safety is at stake, we need to intervene, but knowing when and how can take practice. Sometimes a toddler will give a little push to another child who is in her way, and that is the end of it. At other times, it's plain to see that there is more energy behind the push, and it may signal the beginning of more aggression. Then it may be time to move in closely to the children and squat down on their level. Your peaceful presence may be enough to prevent things from escalating. It may not be necessary to say more than "I don't want you to hit Damon," "I won't let you hit Damon," or "Here's a pillow if you feel like hitting." If one or both children continue trying to hit or push, you may put one hand between them so that it won't be possible for one child to hit or push the other. Let your hand be gentle but resolute — not rigid. As always, it is important to see what the children can manage on their own before intervening, and when it's necessary to intervene, to bring a sense of peacefulness to the situation. Do your best to set limits clearly and calmly, without judgment or alarm. (Setting limits is addressed in more detail in the next chapter.)

Over time there is no need to fight the instinct to intervene, because it starts to feel so unnatural and unhelpful. It is much more fun to see how children resolve their own conflicts. Being part of that process brings a tremendous psychic reward, as it is more stimulating than simply descending on a situation and meting out justice willy-nilly. When I do intervene, it is fun to listen and help them resolve the conflict. It actually frees you from having to decide "what is fair" and allows you to enjoy listening to how kids like to make things right.

— Jacinto Hernandez

What Babies and Toddlers Learn from Playing Together

Babies can derive a lot of pleasure from playing near one another. I once observed a group of four babies at a child care center. This group had been together since they were all very young and had been cared for by the same caregiver during that time. I observed as one baby crawled over toward a low wooden shelf. Within minutes, the three other babies made their way across the room. Two babies were sitting up, leaning against each other, and the other two were right there with them, in a huddle. They migrated around the room, one after another, and clearly derived pleasure and comfort from being near one another.

Empathy is the ability to understand another person's feelings and plays an important role in prosocial and moral behavior. Babies begin to learn about empathy by having opportunities to interact with one another and discovering they can affect others. Young babies don't have a sense of ownership, so when one baby takes an object from another baby's hand, the other baby may take it back or will look around for another object to engage with. Eventually that young baby will grow to become a toddler who *will* complain or cry when another child takes an object from her. Instead of chastising the child who took the object, or asking her to give it back or to share, we look at moments like these as valuable learning opportunities. The child whose object has been plucked away is free to express her emotion and can choose to go after the object to retrieve it, find something else to play with, or hold on tight the next time. In this way, the taker is able to observe and feel how her behavior affects another, and the other child learns something as well—about how much the object means to her in that moment and what she's willing to endure to keep it. Both children also learn about negotiation and compromise. These lessons don't come quickly, but when a child finally learns to wait for her turn or to give an object to another child, this comes from an empathetic and genuine place within the child, rather than being a disingenuous behavior imposed by an adult. If adults are necessary to "keep the peace," what happens when an adult is not around? Toddlers can learn to be empathetic, patient, and kind to one another, but the learning process requires a commitment on the part of adults to set clear and consistent limits, with patience and kindness. We model the behavior we want our children to develop.

When you observe babies and toddlers at play together, it's not necessary to narrate or say anything unless the child looks to you, shows you something, or engages with you, or if you need to intervene for reasons of safety. "You filled the bucket up with balls." "You stacked the cups together. You look very pleased about that!" "It hurt Ethan when you hit the block against his head. If you want to hit, you can hit the block on the floor or on this bucket." "Sara grunted. She doesn't want you to push her. If you want to be with Sara, you can touch her gently." Model gentleness and prosocial behavior and give your child time to internalize the behavior.

Liam continues to impress me with his ability to take in and respond to the behavior of other children. I used to feel a need to protect him when other kids were moving around him. Inversely, I became anxious when Liam asserted his wishes with other kids. In both situations, I have been surprised by his ability to handle the emotional ups and downs of these situations on his own. He may get hurt, frustrated, or sad when another child takes a toy from him. He may watch the other child play with it for a long time. He feels empathy when other kids cry. He is persistent when he wants to do something and someone is in his way. I'm not sure I would have noticed these things if I hadn't been introduced to Educaring. It has taught me to trust what Liam wants for himself over what I think he should do. His intuition and development are the most important things to me.

— Michael Cassidy

WHY PLAY MATTERS

Playtime is a time for exploration and self-initiated activity, not a time for your baby to be entertained, by you or by an overstimulating toy (think TV). When that's the case, a child can quickly lose the thread to her inner curiosity.

A parent's responsibility is to provide an environment that is physically and cognitively challenging, so that the objects are in tune with the baby's interests and abilities. This allows the baby to explore and discover the world on her own, rather than needing an adult to show her how something is to be done. Some challenge is a good thing. Too much challenge can make it difficult, if not impossible, for the baby to engage in her play in any deep way. It's fascinating to observe a baby at play and see her tenaciously resolve a problem on her own.

When I first met Emmi Pikler, I was struck by her innovative theories that made it possible for us to become respectful partners with infants in their care. Her intuitive philosophy, which inspired Magda Gerber's founding of RIE, helps parents become more attuned to their children. This in turn enables them to make a successful transition socially, emotionally, and cognitively into nursery school. RIE continues to be the organization that fosters one of the best starts for a progressive, play-based nursery school experience.

— Timothy Craig, founder of Children's Circle Nursery School

When children are given time and space to play without interruption, they develop skills that will serve them well when it's time to go to school. Some key indicators for success in school are curiosity and confidence, in oneself and others, and the ability to focus, concentrate, pay attention, get along with others, and ask for help. Of course, these are skills that continue to develop and expand as children grow and widen their experiences, but the foundation is laid in the first two years of life. How wonderful for a child to go to school with a curious spirit, with the feeling that exploring and learning about the world are pleasurable experiences. Play, then, is not just a trivial pastime. Babies and toddlers are not idly fiddling about with objects when they play; they're learning how to learn.

7. Learning Limits

Basically, most parents are afraid of disciplining their children because they are afraid of the power struggle. They are afraid of overpowering the child, afraid they will destroy the child's free will and personality. This is an erroneous attitude.

—Magda Gerber, *Dear Parent*

Children learn what is expected of them—and what it is to be human—by observing their parents. This may feel like a weighty responsibility, but it's true. If we want our children to be kind and compassionate, *we* need to be kind and compassionate. If we want them to be patient, we need to work on being patient ourselves. If we have a short fuse, chances are good that our children will have one as well. How many times have you heard a parent holler at a child, "Stop yelling!" But if our children look to us to learn what is socially acceptable, how can we expect them to behave any differently than we do? Children are like mirrors that reflect our best and worst selves back to us. When we see a pattern of behavior that we'd like to change in our child, it's likely there's something we first need to change in ourselves. Our children can be powerful motivators for self-reflection and learning.

Our approach to discipline is largely determined by how we were brought up and by cultural influences. It is also affected by our temperament, life experience, and trust in human nature. Some people believe that babies and young children are like feral animals that need to be tamed. They assume that noise and discord are a necessary part of life with babies and toddlers. They may threaten, scold, shame, or spank their children for even the smallest of infractions. They may bribe or offer rewards in exchange for desired behavior, which is a form of coercion. An authoritarian approach to discipline may get the immediately desired result, but at what cost? Imagine that a toddler clobbers his baby brother, who begins to scream. The mother hollers at the child to go to his room. If he was hitting his brother out of frustration or jealousy, being sent to his room will likely intensify the emotion. What if the mother yanks the toddler away by the arm, spanks his bottom, and says, "Cut it out!"? The mother's violent reaction has done nothing to help her toddler learn to be gentle but only reinforces aggression as an appropriate mode of behavior. The mother's intervention heightens the emotional chaos and affords the toddler no opportunity to observe, take in, and feel how his behavior has affected his brother. It certainly has a negative effect on the child's sense of self and his relationship with his mother as well.

Having said this, it's impossible for any parent to respond evenly and peacefully to undesirable behavior 100 percent of the time. We all have moments when we lose our patience with our children. Ruptures are a natural part of any dynamic human relationship. What is important is the repair that follows the rupture. Be sure to talk to your baby about what happened. "I got really scared when you climbed on the back of the sofa. I yelled." "That startled you, and you cried really hard. I'm sorry I scared you." If you lost it with your toddler and slapped him, talk to him about what happened. Acknowledge your mistake and apologize. "I got mad when you poured your juice on the floor. I hit you. I'm sorry. That was wrong." "Hitting is not a good thing to do, and I will try very hard not to do it again." Wait and give your child time to respond. If your toddler is older and has the language, you can ask him, "How did it make you feel when I hit you?" Give your toddler the opportunity to express his feelings about what happened. Interactions and conversations such as these will help mend the hurt and anger and restore good feelings between you.

When a parent-child relationship is based on mutual respect

and trust, it *is* possible for babies and toddlers to accept limits without difficulty. For those times when limits must be set and a child *does* become upset, the upset is acknowledged and eventually passes. This isn't because the child has learned to be compliant but because limits have been set clearly and consistently in a habitual way and the child has come to know what is expected of him. A toddler was in class with his mother when his father arrived and sat down close to his wife and gave her a kiss. The child burst out crying and demanded that his father move away, across the room from his mother. The father quietly but firmly told his son, "I know you want me to sit over there, but I want to sit next to Mommy." We all listened as his son cried in protest for several minutes, but then he was done. He picked up a bucket in one hand and a basket in another and returned to his play.

Instead of *controlling* your baby or toddler, act as his guide — let him know what you expect, set firm boundaries with compassion for his point of view, and trust that, over time, he will learn what is expected of him. When you trust in your child's innate goodness and understand that self-discipline takes practice, you'll be willing to set the same limit several times a day, for many days if necessary, until your child begins to have the self-control to manage an impulse. Instead of punishing him for behavior you're not in favor of, calmly let him know what you expect. Stating what you want in a positive way, in a tone that reflects your confidence that he will cooperate, will help keep things from devolving into a power struggle. Rather than saying, "Put the stool down!" in a punitive, shaming, or authoritarian voice, simply say, "The stool stays on the floor." Instead of "You know you can't climb on the counter," offer a more constructive alternative by saying something like "I

won't let you climb here, but you can climb on the steps."
Remind yourself that all good habits take time to establish and
sometimes need to be reinforced. When we bark in anger, it
creates hurt and shame, and a rift between parent and child.
It's hurtful and shaming to yell, "How many times do I have to
tell you to put your truck away when you're done playing with
it?" It can be a relief to discover that by stating the facts—"I
see a truck on the stairs"—we can get the desired result while
keeping good feelings intact. It is also likely that your toddler
will *want* to cooperate in response to your simple observation
rather than being shamed, bullied, or frightened into comply-
ing with your demands.

When parents set a limit and their toddler responds in
upset or anger, they sometimes think they've failed to set the
limit in the "right" way or say the magic words that would
prompt their child to comply without difficulty. That's an
unrealistic expectation. There will be times when you set a
limit and your child will become upset. Hold fast and remain
calm. There will be times when you set a limit and it will be
ignored altogether. These are both to be expected from a
growing toddler, who is merely exercising his power and test-
ing the limits, so refrain from characterizing this as *mis*behavior. Having said that, it's important to set a limit and follow
through with it rather than giving your child multiple chances
to comply. When we do that, the child learns that we don't
really mean what we say, and when we let things go on too
long, we can find ourselves feeling angry and ready to explode.
It's preferable to state a limit once, give the child time to comply, and then follow through with it before we lose our patience.
As RIE Associate Janet Lansbury states, "[The child] may
squawk in response, or even have a meltdown, but she will also

breathe a huge inward sigh of relief.... Taking care of yourself and your child—prioritizing your relationship to this extent— is the ultimate in great parenting and something to feel extremely proud of. Children don't want to be considered bothersome, frustrating, or annoying and they don't deserve our resentment. But only *we* can set the limits necessary (and early enough) to prevent these feelings from cropping up and poisoning our relationship."[1]

WHY SETTING LIMITS IS IMPORTANT

It's impossible to be happy and content all the time, yet many parents believe they should do whatever it takes to prevent their babies and toddlers from being disappointed or unhappy. These parents are uncomfortable saying no and can't tolerate their child's real or potential upset. They hurt when their babies cry and do whatever they can to accommodate their toddler's desires so as to avoid their child's disappointment, tears, or angry outburst. This creates an unrealistic expectation in the child and sets him up for confusion and disappointment when he later discovers that the world will not oblige his every whim. Indulged, entitled children are seldom cheerful, often whiny, and very difficult to live with. They've learned to believe that the world revolves around them, and they need only whine, yell, or stomp their feet to get what they want. Their parents haven't given them the opportunity to discover and cope with the fact that life involves struggle, disappointment, and compromise.

Setting limits for your child isn't punitive when it's done in a direct, respectful, and compassionate way. As Magda said,

"Lack of discipline is not kindness...it is neglect."[2] Acknowledge your child's point of view while letting him know the boundaries beyond which he cannot go. Without a parent setting firm boundaries, an out-of-control toddler can feel that he's the most powerful one in the room, and this can be frightening for him. When limits are few and far between, or when a parent repeatedly gives in to a toddler, he will push harder and harder, perhaps having an unconscious desire for the adult to step up to the plate and take charge. Setting firm and consistent limits facilitates the child's sense of security. It helps a child learn what is expected of him and to internalize limits, thereby creating *habits* of socially acceptable and appropriate behavior that provide a secure framework within which a child is free to be himself.

Don't wait until your child is walking to begin to set limits; start when he's a very young baby. It may seem playful and cute when he crawls onto your lap and tries to pull your glasses off your face, but glasses aren't play objects, so why not set a clear limit that they're not to be touched? Saying, "I don't want you to touch my glasses," as you put your hand between your baby's hand and your face sends a clear message. You can't do without your glasses, of course, but you may opt not to wear jewelry that will be attractive to your baby, who may want to explore it. Let's say your baby is curious about your necklace. Touching it is harmless, but what about when he starts to pull on it? You may put your hand over your necklace so that he can't touch it, and kindly say, "I don't want you to pull on my necklace." You may have to repeat these limits many times, of course. Self-discipline doesn't happen instantaneously; it develops over time.

Even for parents who have difficulty setting limits, doing

so can be easy when safety is at stake. If your toddler escapes from your grip and starts to run toward the street, you'll run after him and set a limit in no uncertain terms. Magda referred to this as a red light situation. You don't stop to think or ponder how to respond. You instinctively do whatever is necessary to protect your child's safety, and you do it immediately. But what about those other times when the situation is less clear? A yellow light situation is more ambiguous and is subject to possible negotiation. It happens when you and your child want two different things. Your baby is playing peacefully in his safe space while you're sitting nearby. You're suddenly starving and want to go to the kitchen to make something to eat. You come close, get down on your baby's level, and tell him that you're going to the kitchen and will be back in a few minutes. But when you stand up to leave the room, he starts to wail. Now what do you do? Stay with him or go to the kitchen to grab a bite to eat? Give in to your baby's wishes or do what you'd like to do? At times like these, many parents feel ambivalent and unsure about how to proceed. You might feel yourself wavering and think, "Well, I guess I can wait to eat until he has his nap." But when we repeatedly give in to our baby's every upset and ignore our own needs, we can become angry and resentful. It's essential to take care of ourselves before we get to that point.

To build a relationship based on *mutual* respect and consideration, it's important to listen to what you want or need to do for yourself in the moment; when you do this, you are practicing and modeling self-respect. When you convey your true, honest feelings to your baby, he will learn that you have needs as well. So how might you respond to your crying baby when all you really want to do is get something to eat? By acknowledging his point of view. "I know you want me to stay here, but I need to get something to eat. I'll be back in a few minutes." Then slowly walk out of the room. There can sometimes be confusion between your baby's needs and his wants or desires in the moment, especially when his protestations are pulling at your heartstrings. Of course, you'll always provide for your baby's *needs*, but it's important for him to learn that he can't always have what he wants, when he wants it. Learning to be patient is a valuable lesson. And, importantly, by leaving your baby alone in his safe space, he can learn to be peacefully on his own for a while.

When we give in to every upset, we deprive babies of the process of *self*-discovery and the opportunity to learn to be self-reliant. To care for your baby happily and well, you must be sure to take care of your own needs. As Magda said, "It helps to be strongly attuned to our own inner-rhythm—to know what your needs are, and to convey these to your family so they learn to respect your needs, too. Continuing to sacrifice your own needs for the child's can create inward anger within both of you."[3]

It will be easier for your baby to accept yellow light disappointments when there are plenty of green light times during the day. A green light is given when you've offered your child a few options from which to choose, and you're happy and willing to do any of them. "Would you like to go to the park or play in the backyard?"

To live happily and peacefully within your family and within your child's larger community, he has to learn socially acceptable behavior. Over time, he'll learn how to communicate with others and assert his point of view respectfully. He'll develop empathy for others and begin to learn the art of compromise and negotiation. Children don't come into the world knowing what's acceptable and what's not, and the process of learning can be messy and fraught with emotion. It's important to have realistic expectations for each stage of your baby's development. It would be silly to tell a ten-month-old baby not to mouth an object, and equally silly to expect a toddler to sit quietly in one place when he prefers to walk and run to explore his world. When you understand and trust in a baby's natural development, you can have appropriate expectations and respond to your child accordingly.

WHEN TO WAIT AND WHEN TO INTERVENE

Babies and toddlers learn how to live peacefully with one another by having opportunities to interact with other familiar babies and toddlers, with an attentive adult nearby to provide emotional support and ensure physical safety. When parents attend classes with their babies and toddlers, it's important that the group size is small—ideally, not more than four or five for a young baby or six or seven for a toddler. When a group is larger, it can be overstimulating for a child. It's also important for the group to be predictable, meaning that it's the same, consistent group of babies and toddlers each time. Large classes of fifteen to twenty, with an ever-changing cast of characters, are not ideal situations for babies or toddlers, who thrive on familiarity and routine.

When babies and toddlers interact with one another, their interactions are sometimes awkward and emotional; this is all part of the process of learning. A young baby doesn't become upset when another baby takes an object from him. He may immediately retrieve the object, and a back-and-forth exchange can go on for some time. Or the baby may look for another object to play with. Upset *can* happen in young babies when one baby touches another roughly and surprises or hurts him. Conflict between toddlers, however, most often occurs when both want the same play object.

We do children a disservice when we move in quickly to intervene and try to smooth out all the wrinkles. Conflict and struggle are informative. Babies and toddlers learn about themselves and each other through conflict. They discover how their behavior affects another child, causing him to be amused, upset, or anxious. Your young toddler may pluck an object from another's hands, causing the other child to erupt in a gale of tears. He may stand there and observe the crying child with curiosity and, just when things quiet down, may turn around and take a play object from another child, much to your horror. Perhaps it thrills him to experience the sense of power he has over another child. Or he might be acting as a scientist would, trying to understand emotional cause and effect, and finding out what all the fuss is about.

Just as you don't rush in to rescue a baby who is losing his balance, refrain from rushing in to mediate a conflict between two toddlers. Trust your toddler to navigate his way through a conflict rather than acting as a referee, negotiator, or problem solver. Being the chief negotiator interferes with a child's ability to learn these important skills themselves. When a conflict happens between two toddlers, pay close attention, do your best to wait to see what they can handle on their own, and be ready to move in if necessary to intervene. As Magda said, "Wait as long as you can and then wait a little longer." This is much easier said than done, because observing toddlers in conflict can stir up our own feelings of fear, anxiety, and help-lessness. Knowing when to intervene is an art—not a perfect science—and some days you'll do better than others.

Let toddlers settle minor conflicts on their own whenever possible. If it's necessary to intervene, rather than swooping in to sort things out, start by paying close attention. It's possible that just knowing you're paying attention will offer enough emotional support for the children to work it out on their own. If you're across the room and a tussle ensues over a doll, give the children your attention. If they are focused on each other and the play object, and you have no concern about their safety, stay where you are and continue to observe. If the upset increases and one or both of them look to you, they're letting you know they need more support. In this case, move close to them and squat or sit down on the floor, at the children's level. Do your best to let go of any judgment or anger. Pay attention to your breathing and facial expression. Conflict often dissipates when an adult does nothing more than move in close, so your peaceful presence may help the children to calm. If it doesn't, and one child or both look to you, narrate what's happening, using just a few simple words. "You both want that doll. You're pulling on it." Wait, and wait some more. If the conflict escalates and one child tries to hit or bite another, intervene physically by putting your hand between the children to prevent the hit or bite from meeting its target. Responses such as "I won't let you hit" and "I won't let you bite" are preferable to less direct responses like "Hands are not for hitting" or "We don't bite." Try to let go of any notion of how long the conflict should take to resolve. It will end when it ends.

During a class, I once observed a tug-of-war over a beach ball that went on for fifteen minutes. Two twenty-month-old toddlers pulled and pulled on the ball, sometimes falling over and getting up again. They cried and screeched until one of them let go of the ball, walked away, and picked up another object. He was done. Long before the fifteen minutes were up, I thought, "This has gone on long enough." I was ready for the conflict to be over, but the toddlers weren't. Who was I to judge how long was too long? Conflicts go on until one of the parties decides to change course, compromise, or give up because it's no longer important to them.

Pulling, tugging, and taking objects are natural toddler behavior. If this behavior becomes chronic, however, you need to intervene. What do I mean by chronic? In class, I once had a toddler who, as soon as she walked in the gate, began to move from one child to the next, plucking objects out of each child's hands and observing the reaction. It was clear that she had no interest in the objects but was thrilled by the sense of power and the reaction her behavior elicited. Her mother said that this behavior had begun two weeks earlier and happened at every attempted playdate or visit to the playground. If this kind of persistent behavior happens, shadow your toddler and step in when necessary to help him manage his impulse to take. When he begins to reach for another child's object, put your hand in front of his and say, "I won't let you take Georgia's bucket. She's holding on to it." This protects the other child and lets your child know that he can relax because you will be there to help him control the urge to take when it comes up. With your attentive support, such behavior will eventually disappear.

It can be challenging to remain peaceful with a child who is behaving aggressively because it stirs up our own emotions. If you feel your anger rising, be honest. "I'm *really* frustrated.

You keep taking Quentin's toys, and he's upset." In such instances, it's important for us to model a kinder, gentler way of being and interacting with others. A child who is chronically aggressive needs to see, feel, and hear what it is to be kind and gentle, with others and with himself. Bathe the child in gentleness, again and again.

When setting limits, avoid using the "royal we," which is indirect and can be confusing. If your toddler has just walloped another child and you say, "We don't hit!" he may rightly think, "What do you mean? I just hit her!" Speaking in the first person is direct and lets your child know what your limits are and how you feel about his behavior. It also models how to speak up for yourself. "I don't want you to hit Sascha" or "I won't let you hit Sascha" is much more direct and has an altogether different tone than "We don't hit." It's also very different from "Why do you keep hitting Sascha?" which includes negative judgment and asks a question that your child may not be able to answer.

HAIR PULLING

Perhaps your baby has grabbed hold of your hair and is tugging away on it. As you gently pry his fingers loose, you can say, "I don't want you to pull my hair. That hurts." Don't soften what you're saying with a smile or be playful while you're setting the limit, as this sends a conflicting and confusing message. A child of any age can understand the seriousness of what you're saying by the look on your face and the tone of your voice.

If your baby has crawled over to another baby and pulls her

hair, and you're not already on the floor, get down and move close to the babies. Stroke the back of your baby's hand to loosen his grip or gently pry his fingers open. Stroke each baby's head and say, *"Gentle."* As you do this, narrate the scene. "Gentle, Javier. Lina doesn't like it when you pull her hair." "Gentle. You're upset, Lina. That hurt." For babies whose gripping reflexes have just recently disappeared, and whose fine motor skills are immature, it takes time and practice for them to learn to touch gently. As you narrate, touch each baby's head softly so that both of them can feel what it's like to be touched gently. As Magda Gerber said, "We comfort both children. When we comfort only the victim, the victim is rewarded for being a victim and the aggressor has no opportunity for learning gentleness."

How would you feel if you were angry and frustrated and someone responded by asking you to be gentle? It would probably feel like an emotional mismatch, as if the person was responding to your fury with a feather. Most of us want to feel that whoever is witnessing our upset is really hearing us and accurately reflecting our emotional state back to us. When an older baby or toddler is aggressive, saying "gentle" and touching gently is no longer sufficient. If a toddler has kicked another child and we just touch him softly and say, "Gentle," he now has the power to push our hand away to strike again. Even if a toddler is not speaking a lot of words, he has a much greater capacity to understand than he did when he was a young baby, so we can use more language to address the situation. "I'm putting my hand here. I won't let you kick Tamika. You seem angry. You can kick a ball or the cushion if you want to kick." The limit setting and language we use grow and develop along with the child.

BITING

Few behaviors elicit as much parental concern as biting. But biting is a primal urge and is a natural behavior for some babies and toddlers. Your nursing baby may suddenly bite down on your nipple. Let him know it hurt you—"Ouch!"—and take him off the breast. Some babies bite when they're teething, hungry, tired, or overstimulated. They may bite because it feels good or to get your attention (it will!). If you've nibbled on his toes, your baby may assume that biting is acceptable and not understand the distinction between a nibble and a chomp. Babies may bite to experiment and to see how another person reacts. If that's the case, you may say, "That hurt Jessie. I won't let you bite her. If you want to bite, you can bite on one of these" (offer a choice of two play objects). Toddlers may bite when they don't have sufficient words to express themselves. Biting another child's arm conveys "I'm angry!" quite clearly. You can respond by saying, "You're upset. You can bite these rings or hit the cushion." As always, it's important to respond to both the aggressor and the victim. An empathetic acknowledgment of the bite, without pity, can be sufficient, "Jaden bit you. That hurt."

You may be able to prevent biting by trying to understand what triggers it. Start by asking yourself if your baby's basic needs have been met. Is he hungry or tired? Is he overstimulated? Is he teething? At times the reason will be clear, and at other times you just won't know. If your baby or toddler is with other children, prevent another bite by being attentive and staying close to your child to ensure the safety of the other children. If he comes close to another child and opens his mouth, put your hand between his mouth and the other child to prevent the bite from connecting. You might say, "I won't let you bite." If the child is particularly agitated, you may notice that saying anything only heightens the emotion. If your toddler is biting uncontrollably, holding him tightly may help him to calm, and if he's with other children, it may be necessary to remove him from the situation. Do your best to bring a sense of peacefulness to your child. There may be times when you do everything you can to prevent a bite, but it still happens. In this case, forgive the child and forgive yourself.

HITTING AND PUSHING

At times, your toddler will hit or push just to experiment and see how another child reacts. When this happens, observe to see how the one who is pushed or hit responds. Perhaps she takes it in stride and it's over. If your toddler persists, you'll need to move close to ensure safety. Narrate what you see, set a limit, and provide an appropriate alternative. "It's not okay to hit Hallie. If you want to hit, you can hit the sofa or pillow over there." Your toddler certainly knows the difference between a real person and an inanimate object, so allow him to act out his feelings with his play objects. There may be times when you are able to identify what triggered your toddler to push or hit. Perhaps a toddler is on a ramp, and your child is waiting to climb up it. If the child occupying the ramp is not moving fast enough and your child has insufficient language to say, "Can you hurry up? I want to climb on that, too," a swift push expresses things quite succinctly. Rather than saying, "I don't want you to push," include what you've observed in your response. "It looks like you want to climb up on the cube, too, Will. But it's not safe to push Caroline." "Caroline, Will is waiting to get on the cube." If Caroline continues to linger on the cube and Will grows frustrated, narrate some more for him. "It looks like Caroline is not ready to come down from the cube yet. It's hard to wait." To Caroline, you can say, "Will is looking at you, isn't he? He wants to climb on the cube, too." If Caroline doesn't budge from the cube and Will continues to be frustrated, you might suggest an alternative or see if Will can discover one himself. "Caroline's still on the cube. You can wait until she gets off or find something else to climb on."

WHINING

Toddlers don't whine to make you crazy; they whine to express a need they may not be able to identify or articulate any other way at that moment. Whining serves the purpose of getting your attention. The challenge is for you to keep your cool so that you can try to understand *why* your child is whining. Perhaps a friend is visiting, and you're sitting together on the sofa catching up. Your toddler appears and starts to whine. The common retort, "Stop your whining!" never works. Instead, giving attention to your child for a moment and saying, "I hear you. I'm talking to Diana, and when I'm done, I'll come sit with you," may be all he needs. Of course, it's important to have a reasonable expectation of how long your child can wait to have your full attention. It's not necessary to stop your conversation immediately, but it's unrealistic to expect a toddler to wait for an hour while you chat. If it's just before dinnertime and your toddler starts to whine, then hunger is the obvious cause. Whenever there's whining, just stopping what you're doing and getting down on the floor with your child for a few minutes can help him stop because he'll know that he's been seen and heard.

LABELS ARE LIMITING

Labels are limiting, inaccurate, and often negative. Although they are meant to describe the undesirable *behavior* of a child, they are often used to describe the child as a whole person. "He's a clown." "She's shy." "He's a bully." These words reduce children to less than their complex selves and can cause them to believe what they hear. Labels don't take fatigue, hunger, overstimulation, and the possible emotional overload of interacting with others into account. Instead of saying, "Noah, you're a grouch!" consider why he's behaving the way he is and narrate what you see. "Noah, you're stomping your feet and growling. I wonder why you're upset." Since you can't know for certain what he's feeling, using a nonspecific word like "upset" rather than "mad" or "angry" is more open-ended. Narrating just what you see will help prevent you from making assumptions, keep you from projecting your own issues onto your child, and help you respond accurately to your child's behavior.

Let's say you go to a friend's house, and your toddler sticks like glue to your side, not wanting to explore the play objects. You may feel embarrassed and say, "Raphael is shy," as a way to explain your son's behavior and relieve your embarrassment. Instead, if you feel some tension, perhaps you can release it by speaking to your child. "Raphael, you haven't been to Henry's house in a while."

I once observed a class where a mother walked in with her baby in her arms and announced, "He's a bully." The child wasn't even walking yet, and she was making this proclamation! It seemed as if she was warning the group, "Watch out! Here he comes!" Perhaps it was the mother's way of letting us know that she didn't know how to handle her child's aggressive behavior and needed our help. I wondered what sort of message this sent to her child, who could certainly understand his mother's intonation and expression, if not her words.

CONSEQUENCES VERSUS PUNISHMENT

There may be times when you've set a limit several times, and your child continues to push against it. He may be pushing to be playful or to get a rise out of you. At other times, he may be disregarding the limit you've set. You may want or need to introduce natural consequences, which are not the same as punishment. A consequence happens as a result of your child's behavior. A punishment is a penalty for doing something wrong. Help your baby or toddler learn about cause and effect, or what happens as a result of his actions. These are very different. Your baby pulls up to stand at the gate and drops his plastic keys on the other side. He grunts for you to retrieve them. You may retrieve them once, and he may start to drop them over the gate again. You can kindly say, "It looks like you want to drop your keys over the gate, but I don't want to pick them up anymore. If you drop them over again, you won't have them to play with." If you're at the playground and your toddler continues to throw sand at other children after you've told him it's not safe, give a consequence. Let your words be matter-of-fact but not punitive. "You're having a hard time not throwing the sand. That can hurt the other children. We're going home now, and we can come back to the playground tomorrow." Perhaps you're enjoying spending time at the playground with the other parents. It can be hard to let go of your own agenda to follow through with a consequence, but when you do, you'll be taking an important step to support your child's growing self-discipline. You may have to leave the playground early for several days, but trust that your child will learn the limit. When parents repeatedly set limits without any follow-through, their children learn that they can continue to ignore the limits because they won't be reinforced.

Time Out

When toddlers are emotionally overwrought and out of control, many adults will "put them in time-out." Just when they need a loving adult to help them to regulate, they're banished to a chair in the corner or to their room, alone. "Go to your room until you calm down" is a common directive. It's a penalty that makes no sense. Punishing a child for being out of control doesn't help him to self-regulate. If he spends enough time on the chair or in his room, he may calm, but he will also likely feel shame, hurt, guilt, resentment, anger toward you, or all of the above. Punishment is not an ingredient for a respectful relationship. Rather, a child who is in disequilibrium needs your attention and loving kindness. If your child is screeching and you're at the end of your tether, it's all right to leave him in his safe space and remove yourself from the situation. Speak honestly to him. "You're screaming really loudly, and I'm getting upset. I don't want to yell, so I'm going to my room to calm down. I'll be back in a few minutes." Magda said, "Many parents believe in using time-out. When I hear this expression I always wonder: time out from what? Life? Isn't it better to stay 'in' life and figure out how to do better the next time?"[4]

SHARING

One toddler is playing with a bucket, and another child tugs at it in an attempt to take it for himself. At this point, many adults would ask them to "share nicely." Sharing is a concept that toddlers are too young to understand. The dictionary definition of *share* is to "let somebody use something." But if a child is enjoying playing with an object, asking him to share is essentially asking him to give it up. Why is his desire to play with an object until he's all done less important than another child's desire to play with it? Before he's developmentally ready to share, your child must first have experiences of possessing something, holding on to it, and letting it go when he's ready.

For sharing to come from an authentic and heartfelt place, a child needs to have developed empathy—the ability to understand another's point of view. Empathy develops when a child has opportunities to interact with other children, with the support of an attentive adult. Over time, a child sees how his behavior affects another and has a greater understanding of another child's point of view. Trust that your toddler will develop empathy and that he will take turns or share when he is ready. Most children are not ready to share much before age three, and even then, it can be difficult.

In the meantime, if a friend is coming to your home for a playdate, talk to your toddler beforehand and ask if there are any special play objects that he'd like to put away before his friend arrives. It can be especially difficult, if not impossible, to share our most precious belongings, so let go of any expectation that your toddler will find it easy to allow another child to engage with his play objects.

THE MAGIC WORDS

Parents often wonder about teaching their child good manners. As with all behavior, children learn what they see. If you say "please" and "thank you," your child will learn these social skills when he is ready. Give him time for these words to come from a genuine place rather than coercing him to say them before he is ready. In social situations, a smile, a gentle touch, and a thank-you when your child has managed a social challenge are all that's required. "Thank you for being patient, Joseph." "Lila looks happy that you gave her one of the dolls. Thank you, Nicholas."

As your child grows and develops from toddlerhood and beyond, you will discover that the relationship you have built, based on trust and mutual respect, will serve you well. Although your teenager may balk at your limits with more strength and vigor, the Educaring Approach will give you tools to listen and respond in a way that honors his point of view. You'll see how this respectful approach of being with each other is enduring and applies to all relationships throughout life.

8. Toddlers

*To live with a toddler can, in a funny way, be
therapeutic. All the human anxieties—of feeling good
and bad, loved and abandoned—peak. It is like a ritual
of passage in the journey as a family.*
—Magda Gerber, *Dear Parent*

The magical world of toddlerhood begins when children take their first steps. One of the joys of being with children of this age is the sheer exuberance and enthusiasm they find in even the smallest of things. A toddler may be enthralled as she watches a snail slowly traverse the driveway. She may be absolutely gleeful when she hears the garbage truck approach and downright angry when she can't have what she wants.

Toddlerhood can be a time of high emotion and struggle. The baby who only a short while ago was reliant on you for her every need can now venture out and walk away from you. With a toddler's exhilarating sense of independence comes a new awareness that she is separate from you. This can create turmoil and anxiety for a child. As your toddler exerts her growing autonomy, she will experience the push and pull of wanting to be close to you and wanting to push away to explore the world and assert her independence. She may struggle with these opposing urges simultaneously. Although she can now walk, even run, away from you, don't confuse your toddler's desire to explore as a sign that she needs you any less. Knowing you're there to return to makes it possible for her to venture out happily. Some toddlers will run from their parent's side to investigate a new environment without missing a beat, while others will stay close for a long time before moving away from a parent, if at all. Accept your toddler's choice, whatever it may be. Let her choose if she wants to jump in and when, and refrain from coaxing her to participate if she's not interested or ready to. Your child's temperament will largely determine her response to new people and situations.

Your agreeable and easygoing baby has been replaced by a contrarian with a surprisingly strong point of view. She may demand that Mommy change her diaper. She may order you to sit in one chair rather than another. She may do as my son did and command you to stop singing. Resist the temptation to attach a label to this behavior as bossy or domineering and realize that this phase will pass. Find the humor in it when you can, and respond to your toddler matter-of-factly. Dad, you might say to your toddler, "I know you want Mommy to change your diaper, but Mommy's getting ready for work, so I'm going to change your diaper this time." "I know you want me to sit in that chair, but this is the one I'd like to sit in right now." "You don't want me to sing—but I feel like singing!"

It's natural for your toddler to see how far she can go with issuing commands, and it's your responsibility to provide her with clear and consistent limits, just as you did when she was crawling. She may find it easy to abide by one limit but may find another particularly difficult to adhere to. In this case, you may need to repeat and follow through with that limit for several weeks or months until she is able to internalize it successfully.

There was a twenty-month-old boy in one of my classes who went through a period of hitting any child who came within a foot of him. I shadowed him, staying close by, ready to intervene if necessary. After eight weeks of shadowing, I found myself across the room from him for the first time because I needed to tend to a conflict between two other children. I looked to see that another child had walked close to him. He raised his hand to hit her but then looked over his shoulder to find me. We looked at each other for what seemed like a long time but was probably no more than fifteen seconds, and then he put his hand down. At that moment, I knew that he had finally internalized the limit that I'd been setting for him. Hitting was no longer an issue; he is now a very gentle fourth grader.

OFFERING CHOICES

How do you get a toddler to cooperate? Offering choices can certainly help. When it's time to change a diaper but your toddler wants to continue playing, you can say, "Would you like to walk to the changing table, or shall I carry you?" A few well-placed choices can be offered throughout the day, but try not to overwhelm your toddler with *too many* choices. "Would you like to wear the red shirt or the green one?" "Would you like banana or apple?" "The yellow cup or the blue?" "It's time to leave the playground. Shall we walk to the car or hop like a bunny?" Offering choices gives a child the opportunity to be part of the decision-making process and increases the possibility of cooperation. No one likes to be given orders, and toddlers are no different. It's more respectful to offer choices than to dictatorially tell a child what to do. Choice offering helps a toddler maintain her dignity and may lessen the potential of temper tantrums. A dose of humor and fun may help to encourage cooperation and circumvent a potential upset.

To me the Educaring Approach is about creating communication with my son. To truly respect him, I listen to him by observing, and he is very good at telling me what he needs, wants, sees, and hears, even without any words. I also respect him by speaking to him clearly and honestly about what I expect, need, see, and hear. I am continually thrilled by how we communicate. One morning when he was around seven months old, he crawled out of the kitchen as I was making breakfast. I explained to him that I needed to be able to see him. He could either remain in the kitchen with me or go into his playroom (right off the kitchen). He thought about this for a bit and then returned to play in the kitchen. When I happily told my father the story, I knew that he didn't believe my son really understood.

When he was fourteen months old, I remember explaining to him in a restaurant that the fork could not leave the table, as it was not safe for him to walk around with it. I gave him the option to keep the fork or get down and walk. He chose to put down the fork. My friends at the table looked at me, shocked that he understood and complied, but I was no longer surprised. Now that my son is eighteen months, we hear at least once a week about how smart he must be because he understands everything I say to him. I have to laugh because every child in my son's RIE class understands the same amount. RIE children understand because they were spoken *to*, not at, from a very early age.

— Arianne Groth

The words we choose are important. Closed-ended questions and statements are preferable to wishy-washy, apologetic ones. If you need to get out the door to an appointment, you can say, "It's time for us to go now" rather than "Are you ready to go?" When it's bedtime, saying, "The book is all done. It's time to rest," sets a clear limit that lets a child know it's time to go to bed. Try to do away with "okay?" at the end of sentences. Perhaps parents use this word to soften a statement or direc-

tion or make it sound friendlier. But speaking in a nonaffirma-
tive way can be confusing to a child and does little to elicit
cooperation. When a parent says, "It's time to go home now,
okay?" a toddler often responds by saying, "No!" In this con-
text, the word "okay" is disingenuous and sends a message that
what has been said is somehow up for negotiation. It just begs a
child to be contrary. Instead, state the facts. "It's time for us to
go home. I'm going to the living room to get my keys. When I
get back, it will be time to put on your shoes." Since time is an
abstract concept for a toddler, having a visual cue—"When I
get back"—can help her to understand what happens next.
Your toddler may be upset, or not. If she is, you can speak to
her about it and let her know that she has been seen and understood. "You're upset. You've been having so much fun playing
with Graham, and it's hard to leave. But it's time to go home
for a rest now. We'll see Graham tomorrow."

Billy gets to choose his bibs, socks, shoes, and shirts. We also
give him a choice when he is resisting doing something. For
example, if he doesn't want to go up the stairs to go home and
wants to run down the path instead, I'll ask him if he wants me
to carry him or if he'd like to walk up the stairs himself. He may
take a moment, think about it, and then let me know what he
wants to do. Giving him a choice helps him have some control
over his circumstance.

— Natascha Corrigan Aldridge

Just as you did when she was a baby, narrate what is happening or about to happen, give your toddler tarry time to
prepare, and *wait* for her cue that she's ready. Toddlers are

often misinterpreted as being uncooperative when it's just that life is moving too quickly, and they can't keep up with the pace. As soon as toddlers can walk and run, parents mistakenly believe they can speed up, but this isn't true. Slowing down can provide a sense of peacefulness for a sometimes-overwhelmed toddler. When life continues to move slowly, with transitions that are few and predictable, your toddler will be better able to stay on an even keel.

Keeping up with a toddler can be physically and emotionally exhausting. Toddlers seem to be in constant motion as they explore their world. They climb, squat, walk, run, and find sheer joy and pleasure in movement. After a long day, it may be impossible to calmly and consistently set limits, so forgive yourself if you sometimes give in. If you find yourself in the middle of setting a limit and suddenly realize it's not that important to you, it's okay to just let it go. You know the saying "Choose your battles?" It's true. Sometimes, in midsentence, you may decide to change course. "I said we needed to leave the park now, but I changed my mind. I can go to the store later, so we can stay for a little while longer." Sometimes we discover that what we thought was important is, in fact, not, at least in that particular moment. As long as it's not a red light situation where safety is at stake, it's okay to adjust our course from time to time. Being flexible and forgiving, of ourselves and others, is a good example to set for our children.

Of course, some limits are nonnegotiable, and issues of safety top the list. A toddler's ability to explore expands with her new ability to walk, climb, and run. What may have been out of reach a few months ago may be easily accessible now. She can push a stool over to the kitchen counter to climb into the sink and turn on the hot water or extract a sharp knife from its holder. Take a look around your home to be sure that everything is safe and any potential dangers are out of reach. Toddlers have expansive ideas, and it's much more pleasurable for them to be able to follow through with those ideas in a safe environment that supports their curious explorations rather than inhibits them.

The nonnegotiables in our house mostly have to do with climbing, as Liam likes to climb. We don't want him to climb on the tables or bookshelves. We don't want him to play with the dog's water bowl or the oven and stove. We want him to eat at the table. We want him to stay seated while he eats. We want him to treat the dog kindly. Pretty much everything else is up for discussion.

— Michael Cassidy

ACKNOWLEDGE YOUR TODDLER'S WORDS AND FEELINGS

It's important to let your toddler express her feelings, whether she's happy, sad, frustrated, or angry, no matter how irrational that feeling may seem to you. If your child is terrified of the neighbor's friendly dog, accept her emotional reality. Chances are good she won't be frightened of dogs forever. Rather than saying, "It's okay. Don't be scared. He's a nice dog. He won't hurt you," just acknowledge your toddler's feelings. "You seem scared. The dog is behind the fence, and he can't get out. Would you like to hold my hand, or do you want to walk on your own?" If she's upset because you've told her she can't play with your phone, let her express how she feels. Saying, "You know you can't play with my phone, so why are you angry?" is of little consequence to your toddler, who lives in the moment. She wants to play with your phone, and she wants it now. Your patience may be tested as you acknowledge her upset: "You're angry because you want to play with my phone. But it's not a play object."

We live in a town house with a common driveway with the other units. When my sons were in a stroller and we'd walk down the driveway, we'd have to pass by "Number One's house," as my sons would call it. We would see this man, who used to be an opera singer, sitting in his garage with the door open. He would break into song as we passed by. Jackson was afraid of his appearance and booming voice, yet there was no other way around his unit. One day Jackson, who loves the park, did not want to go. When I asked him why, he said that when we passed by Number One's garage and saw him, it scared him. I asked Jackson if there was anything I could do to make him feel safe. Jackson asked me if I would lower the hood on the double stroller and place a blanket over it so that he could not see Number One and Number One could not see him. Jackson found a solution that worked for him. For quite a while, until Jackson felt comfortable passing by Number One, we would always leave the house with a blanket over his side of the stroller.

— Jill Getto Lee, RIE Associate

It is much easier to accept a child's emotional state than to try to squelch her feelings or encourage her to feel another way. This only compounds the upset because a child feels unheard and abandoned right when she needs us the most.

"You're okay. You didn't hurt yourself." "Don't be silly." "It's no big deal." These phrases and their many variations only add fuel to the emotional fire because for a toddler, whatever she's upset about *is* a big deal! Now, added to the initial upset is the further upset of you trying to jolly or talk her out of it or negate her feelings altogether. This only teaches your child that certain emotions are permissible and others are not. She may choose to suppress or shut down certain feelings altogether, and as we all know, this can lead to physical and emotional difficulties down the road. Let your toddler know that it's okay to express her full range of emotions. Let the emotions run their course and stay close until the upset has ended.

One day my son bumped his head on the dining-room table as I sat there with three friends. All the friends were parents, and immediately, before he even had time to react, they began trying to pacify him. One friend said, "Brush it off! Brush it off!" while another chimed in with the usual "It's okay! It's okay!" My son looked at me, and I said, "I see you bumped your head on the corner of the table. You're taller now and can hit your head." He touched the table corner and then his head and then continued to play. My friends commented that he was such a relaxed kid, but I knew that my son craved the acknowledgment of his experience, and when I provided that, he could move on.

— Arianne Groth

TALKING TODDLERS

Your toddler will talk and start to acquire language with amazing speed sometime between the ages of one and three. Much of the language will be used to assert her growing autonomy: "Mine!" "Move!" "No!" This is all a natural part of your toddler's drive to assert her independence. The same principles of narrating still apply. Continue to speak in short sentences, using simple words to let your toddler know what's happening or what's about to happen next. Give time for her to respond to you, and don't be concerned if she uses the wrong words. If she points to a photo of a donkey and says, "Horse!" there's no need to correct her. In time, she'll be able to make the distinction. Don't embarrass or shame her by laughing if she uses a wrong word or mispronounces it. Doing so may inhibit her desire to speak. When your toddler says something to you that you can't understand, let her know. "You're trying so hard to tell me something, but I don't understand." Communication should be a pleasure. Relax, knowing that your toddler will speak and add more words to her vocabulary when she is ready.

TANTRUMS

Your child's temperament will largely determine whether or not she has tantrums and how often they occur. Parents who practice the Educaring Approach often report that their children have few tantrums, and when they do, the parents are usually able to understand what triggered it. When life is predictable, and when children are given time to prepare for transitions and their points of view are acknowledged, tantrums may happen far less frequently.

A tantrum is not a demanding outburst or a moment of anger. It's a tidal wave of emotion that overtakes a toddler that can't be circumvented or stopped. How long will it last? Until it's done. Your toddler may kick, scream, cry, hit, bite, wail, or lie on the floor—often in public. Why? Sometimes tantrums are the result of hunger, fatigue, or overstimulation. Hunger and fatigue may be relatively easy to avoid, but overstimulation can sneak up on you. Maybe friends or grandparents are visiting and have been coaxing your toddler to interact with them all day. Perhaps your child accompanied you on several errands this afternoon, or you're in a frazzle and have had no time to give her your full attention. These kinds of situations can be emotionally challenging for a toddler, and a tantrum can serve to release pent-up energy, so that the child feels refreshed when the tantrum is over. Other tantrums seem to come out of the blue. Maybe you've made the unforgivable mistake of serving pear instead of apple juice, or you served it in the smooth glass instead of the bumpy one. Tantrums can happen when you set a limit that thwarts your toddler's expansive plans. If she had the language skills to explain herself, your toddler might respond to your limits with words—"I *want* to pull the cereal boxes down from the grocery shelf!" "I don't want to go to the post office with you. I want to stay *home!*" "I *want* those cookies by the cash register." Tantrums can also happen when your toddler's grandiose ideas are met with skills inadequate to accomplish the task she has in mind. Perhaps your toddler wants to zip her sweatshirt herself and will accept no offer of assistance. When her valiant effort doesn't produce the desired result, her frustration may erupt in a tantrum.

How do we respond to a child who is having a tantrum? As Magda said, children who are having an emotional upset don't need a time-out; they need a "time-in" with us to provide them with emotional and sometimes physical support. There's no one-size-fits-all response to every situation, but however you *do* respond, do so with compassion. If you're feeling angry that your toddler's tantrum interrupted your work or what you hoped would be a fun time together, your emotions will only heighten the already charged atmosphere. Take a few breaths, try to calm yourself, and then stay close to your child until her tantrum is over. If she's hitting or biting you or another child, you will need to intervene immediately. Some children don't want to be touched or held when they're having a tantrum. This is fine as long as they're not hurting themselves, other people, or any objects that may be within reach, but stay close until the tantrum has ended. At other times, you may need to contain your kicking toddler in your arms to protect others or the environment. Holding a child tightly may help her to organize and calm, whether she's having a tantrum or an angry and aggressive outburst. You can sit behind your toddler on the floor and encircle her flailing body with your arms and legs. Notice if containing her loosely helps her to calm or if a tighter hold is necessary. Observe your child to see what helps her the most. You won't need to look your child in the eyes to know when the tantrum has ended; you will be able to feel her body eventually relax.

If you're in public, you may want to carry your toddler to a more private area or away from the action until her tantrum ends. If you're at the grocery store, you may choose to carry her to the car. If she has a tantrum at the playground, is there a quiet corner you can take her to? Your toddler has built up a well of emotion that needs to be released. Stay present but don't try to appeal to her to calm down, be quiet, or feel other than she's feeling. You might say, "You're mad because I got out the blue pajamas and you want to wear the red ones." When you have no idea what triggered the tantrum, you might simply say, "You're *so* upset." If you realize that hunger is the likely cause of your toddler's emotional outburst, you might say, "It seems like you're really hungry. When you're ready, you can have some apple and cheese." Do your best to provide a peaceful and compassionate presence and stay with your child until the emotion runs its course. Your toddler may be exhausted after a particularly lengthy tantrum, so don't be surprised if she needs a nap or to go to bed earlier that evening.

SNACKS AND MEALTIMES

Toddlers not only eat three meals a day but will also be hungry for snacks in between. Some toddlers "graze" throughout the day, eating about the same amount of food each time they come to the table. Some are adventurous in what they will eat, while others are very choosy. Those who once ate anything put in front of them may suddenly reject certain foods because of their texture, color, or smell. Your toddler may refuse pieces of roast chicken but quite happily eat chicken meatballs. She may gobble down sweet potatoes one day and reject them the next. She may scream if you serve her yogurt in the wrong bowl, or cry if the beans come in contact with the rice on her plate. Take a deep breath and do your best to remain calm. Instead of telling her that it's silly to be concerned about these things, ask her which bowl she'd like for her yogurt and opt to use a divided plate with a separate section for each food item.

When planning a meal for your toddler, it can be helpful to offer at least one food that you think she will enjoy. If she surprises you by rejecting everything, you can tell her that this is the food you have prepared for her, and if she doesn't want it, you will put it away, and she can eat later. Resist the temptation to go back into the kitchen to prepare something else, and trust that if your toddler is hungry, she will eat. She will not starve herself! If you are nervous that your child is not eating enough, keep a record of what she eats at each meal. Do this for a week, and you may be surprised to see that she has eaten much more than you imagined.

If you find yourself trying to control mealtimes by coaxing or bribing your toddler to eat, take a step back and remind yourself that your task is to provide healthy food, and it's up to your child to decide whether or not she will eat, and how much. If your toddler senses your anxiety about her eating, or if you try to force her to eat, it's more than likely that she will resist. It can be difficult, but do your best to maintain a mealtime that is calm and relaxed.

TOILET LEARNING

Toddlers don't need to be trained to use the toilet. When they're ready, they can learn to use the toilet without difficulty. Encouraging, coaxing, or trying to teach your child is unnecessary. Cajoling, bribes, and rewards are unadvisable. All of this can create anxiety and resistance, so instead relax and observe for signs of readiness. Remember that all children eventually learn to use the toilet, and whether your toddler learns sooner rather than later is of little consequence.

How can you tell if your toddler is ready to use the toilet? First, your toddler must be *physically* ready, so that she's able to control her bladder and bowels until she gets to the toilet. If her diaper is always dry in the morning, this is one sign that she may be ready. She must be *cognitively* ready as well—able to understand the process and what she must do to use the toilet. If she has watched you, a sibling, or other children in day care use the toilet, this can be a strong motivator, and she may want to use it, too. She may use it once and then not again for six months. Perhaps this was just a little experiment, but she's not ready to use the toilet routinely. Your toddler may say, "Poop," to let you know that she's defecated, or she may tell you she needs to poop and ask you to go with her to the bathroom. This lets you know that she's aware of her bowel movements in a way that she wasn't at an earlier stage. Your toddler must also be *emotionally* ready as well—able to stop what she's doing to use the toilet rather than eliminating into a diaper.

When your child begins to show interest—by watching you use the toilet or by talking about it—follow her lead. If she wants to flush the toilet for you, let her. She will begin to become familiar with the routine before she is ready to try it herself. When she shows interest, put a potty chair in the bathroom so that it's available if she wants to use it. A potty chair allows a child to have both feet on the ground and not be concerned with maintaining balance while sitting on it. Some parents prefer to use child toilet seats that fit on top of the regular toilet. If you opt for one of these, be sure to have a stool handy so that your child can climb onto the toilet seat herself. Some children are comfortable sitting on a regular toilet seat and leaning slightly forward or holding on to the sides of the seat to maintain their balance. The choice of potty seat, child-size toilet seat, or none at all is best made by observing your toddler to be sure that she's able to relax and comfortably maintain her balance.

You can support the toilet-learning process by dressing your toddler in clothing that she can pull down easily by herself. Leggings, shorts, or pants with elastic waistbands are best. Just as you did when you diapered her, encourage your toddler to be an *active participant* by doing as much as she can on her own, with you nearby to give emotional support and to lend a hand when needed. Instead of pulling down her pants and placing her on the toilet seat, let her pull down her pants and get onto the toilet seat herself. It may take her a while to tear off a piece of toilet paper and wipe her bottom, but if you always do it for her, how will she learn? In the beginning, you may need to help her to wipe thoroughly, or she may need your assistance to pull up her pants. Do as little as you can to assist so that she can practice and do what she can when she's ready. If she's in a hurry to urinate, she may need your assistance to pull down her pants. Maybe next time she'll notice the urge to urinate before time is about to run out, and will be able to pull down her pants herself. Some toddlers become upset when they see their feces disappearing down the toilet, so don't force your child to flush the toilet if she doesn't want to. It's important to remember that it's all about readiness, so don't push anything that your toddler resists or doesn't seem ready for. The final part of the toileting routine is washing hands when finished. Have a stool nearby so that she can wash her hands in the sink.

When toddlers are engaged in an activity, they may miss or ignore their body's cues. Although your toddler may not want to stop what she's doing to use the toilet, she may discover that when she sits on the toilet, she *does* have to urinate. Accidents will happen, especially in the first few weeks. This is natural. If they persist longer than that, it's possible that your toddler isn't ready. When your child has an accident, don't make a fuss. Don't shame or scold. You can simply say, "Your underpants are wet. Let's change them." If your toddler wets the bed during the night, you may want to double-sheet the mattress, using two waterproof cloths or covers — one on top of the mattress and one between the two sheets. That way, if the top sheet becomes wet, you can simply remove it along with the waterproof cover, revealing the fresh sheet below. This will keep the mattress from getting wet and save you from having to make the bed from scratch in the middle of the night. Throughout the toilet-learning process, the adult's role should be one of patient and gentle supportiveness. Learning to use the toilet takes practice.

When you live with a toddler, there will be days when it seems you witness every human emotion in the space of an hour, or less. Your toddler may be overjoyed one moment and full of despair the next. She may be enjoying a meal quite happily and suddenly scream that she doesn't like the color of the plate or her food. Your child has a growing ability to assert her point of view, with vocal enthusiasm. "Mine," "No," and "I want it" are common refrains. However much this is true, toddlerhood also brings a unique sense of wonder and sheer delight. It's a gift to spend time with toddlers, who can remind us to appreciate the little things that we might otherwise miss.

9. As Your Baby and Family Grow

*The most important thing to remember is that changes
in your child's behavior are not "setbacks" but are simply
part of her ongoing growth and development.*
—Magda Gerber, *Dear Parent*

Just when you think you've finally figured things out—your baby's sleeping schedule, his food preferences, what helps to soothe him—he changes! The baby who slept peacefully through the night is now waking and demanding your attention. The sweet potatoes he loved only last week are now summarily rejected. Your baby is not being stubborn or contrary. These changes are just part of his natural growth and development. Try to let go of what worked yesterday and do your best to adapt flexibly to your baby as he grows. Magda Gerber said that "the first few years of life are filled with continuing cycles of disequilibrium–adaption–harmony. For parents, it means continually adapting to new developments."[1] Knowing what to expect at various stages of your baby's development can help you respond to changes with confidence and ease.

SEPARATION AND STRANGER ANXIETY

Sometime in the last quarter of your baby's first year, he will become aware of himself as a separate person and will likely experience separation anxiety, which will manifest in the form of clinginess or distress when you go out of sight. This is a normal stage of development and a result of healthy attachment. Some people may advise distracting your baby so that you can sneak out of the house unnoticed. But doing this will only increase his anxiety because he will never be able to relax and trust that you won't suddenly disappear at any moment. Instead, always tell your baby that you are leaving and acknowledge his emotions. "I can see that you're upset, but I need to go to the store. Maleika is here with you. I'll be back soon." There may be times when he clings to your leg and sobs as you try to leave. At this point, some parents feel so guilty and concerned that they stop to try to soothe their child, hoping he'll calm before they go. But this only prolongs the inevitable leave-taking and can make things even more difficult. The fact is that separation can be painful, and if you are the one who is leaving, you can't also be the one to comfort your baby. As long as another familiar and sensitive adult is there to care for him when you leave, your child will most often be able to learn to tolerate your departures. If you find yourself upset and worried after you leave, you might ask your caregiver to send you a text to let you know that your child has recovered, just to set your mind at ease. When you return, you can say, "I came back," and in time your baby will learn to trust that you go but always come back. As he gains more experience with your leaving and returning, he can learn to manage the separation, and his anxiety will lessen until eventually he is able to take your departures in stride.

At the same time that your baby experiences separation anxiety, he may also become anxious around unfamiliar people or in novel situations. Don't try to distract him from his feelings or coax him to interact with an unknown person or venture out in a new environment if he does not want to. Instead, respond sensitively by acknowledging his upset. "Jack's grandma came very close. She touched your hair. You didn't like that." Do your best to advocate for your baby whenever necessary and try to help the adult to understand that your baby may need some time to warm up to a stranger. You might say, "Let's wait and see what he'd like to do." In this way, you are including both the adult and the child.

A NEW BABY

When parents consider having another baby, they sometimes have concerns about how their first child will react. How do you continue to implement the Educaring Approach with two or more and accommodate the needs of more than one child? Respectfully, of course.

If your first child is less than two years of age, the idea of a new baby will be largely abstract, and there is little you can do to prepare him for the change that is to come. He may see Mom's belly swell, but he won't be able to comprehend what it all means. If he has the opportunity to spend time with young babies, a new sibling may seem somewhat familiar to him, but the notion of a new baby living in the house 24/7 may take considerable adjustment.

If he can speak, don't be surprised if your child asks, "Can we give her back now?" once the novelty of the new baby wears off. Yesterday he had you all to himself; today he has to share you with a wrinkly, crying baby. The initial sense of excitement may be supplanted by a profound sense of loss and longing for what was. It is only natural that he may feel jealous of, and angry at, the person who has stolen so much of your attention. If your child is walking and talking, he may regress to crawling and speaking in "baby talk." He may act out by hitting you or his baby sister. Narrate what you see. "Nina's hungry, so I'm nursing her. You're hitting me, and that hurts. I want you to stop." "I know you want to be with me, and it's hard to wait." "Are you upset because you want my attention? When Nina's all done, I'll change her and lay her down for a rest. Then I'll be just with you." This is very different from denying your child's feelings to encourage him to accept his sibling interloper: "Why are you hitting me? You're so lucky to have a baby sister! I know you love Nina!" Just as we allow a child to express his feelings by letting him cry until he's all done, let your child express any anguish he feels about his new sibling, and don't try to encourage him to feel differently.

Many parents have told me they feel guilty about not being able to give their second or third child as much time and attention as the first and that it's difficult to implement the RIE principles all the time. Your toddler may suddenly want your attention just as you sit down to give your baby a bottle. Let him know that you're feeding his sister and will give him your attention as soon as you're done. He can learn to wait, knowing that when it's his turn, he will get your undivided attention.

Finding together time with each of your children, when they have you all to themselves, is very important and can help to ease the transition when a new baby arrives. Your older child can learn that when it's his sister's morning nap time, you will spend some wants nothing time just with him. Once you establish a rhythm with your new baby, it will be easier to identify times throughout the day that you can devote to being with your older child. This one-on-one time will be important to both of you.

MULTIPLES

As you observe and get to know each of your multiple babies, you will learn just how different they are from one another. It is important to interact with multiples in a way that recognizes them as individuals rather than as "the twins" or "the triplets."

Each baby has his own distinct temperament and interests, and each will develop at his own pace. Try not to compare, and take pleasure in each baby's uniqueness.

Dressing multiples in different outfits not only establishes them as distinct people but helps family and friends to identify them, particularly in the beginning, when some people may have difficulty distinguishing one baby from another. Likewise, calling the babies by their names reinforces their individuality and is respectful. My colleague Jill Getto Lee has separate birthday parties for her twin sons on different days. She arranges separate playdates for each of them, so they each have opportunities to play and establish relationships with other children. While they enjoy a special closeness with each other, it is important for them to be able to also enjoy being apart.

When expecting multiples, some parents wonder how they will possibly care for two (or more) babies. How will they meet the needs of their multiple babies all at once? The answer is they won't be able to. Babies can learn to wait. It is far better for a baby to wait a few minutes to eat so that he can later enjoy your full and undivided attention rather than be fed at the same time that you're feeding another child. When multiple babies are fed simultaneously, it more closely resembles an efficient assembly line than an intimate human interaction.

In the hospital, I was instructed to breast-feed both babies at one time. It was challenging because each of my babies latched on differently and had different eating patterns. One would be done very quickly, but his brother often needed to nurse for another ten minutes.

When we got home from the hospital, I continued to try to breast-feed the babies together, but it just made me sad. The "group" breast-feeding experience prevented me from giving my full attention to either baby. Before they were born, I had been told that parents of multiples can lose a lot of bonding time with their babies, and it seemed to be happening to us. But then I thought, "This is not working. There must be something I can do."

I decided to feed one baby at a time, one after the other, and it was a huge relief. When it was time to nurse, I carried each baby to his crib. Then I pulled the rocking chair close to the crib of the baby who would not be fed first so that I could be physically close to him as I fed his brother. After that, it would be time to nurse the first baby. If the baby in the crib began to scream because he was hungry, I would take my attention from the nursing baby for just a moment to talk to the other. "As soon as I'm done feeding William, I will feed you." Both babies learned to trust and wait, knowing their turn would come. Since William latched on and nursed quickly, he was usually the first one to be fed. Then Jackson could enjoy nursing at his usual leisurely pace.

— Jill Getto Lee, RIE Associate

Parents of multiples are often stymied by sleeping arrangements. One crib or two? Does each baby need a bedroom, or can they be in the same room? For all those parents of multiples who don't live in a six-bedroom house, take heart! According to Shelly Vaziri Flais, a pediatrician and mother of twins, "In the early days after coming home from the hospital, many twin newborns are comforted by their twin's presence nearby. As they get bigger and squirmier, though, they will need their own crib space."[2] Although multiples will need their own cribs, parents are sometimes surprised to learn that their babies can sleep in the same room, and one baby will not disturb the sleep of another. In fact, multiples are so familiar and attuned to one another that being together can actually provide comfort and security. They learn to tune out sounds that the other is making—it's just a familiar part of the background noise.

When both of my sons were babies, they had separate cribs up against one wall, head to foot, in one room. One night Jackson was standing up, holding on to the side of his crib and crying, while William was sleeping in his crib. On the video monitor, I watched as William woke up and slowly rose to standing. He looked over the foot of his crib at Jackson, who continued to cry. It seemed clear that William wanted to sleep, but he started to babble and make all kinds of sounds while leaning over the foot of his crib and looking at Jackson. I watched as William emphatically communicated to Jackson in this way. Jackson became still, slowly lowered himself down the side of the crib, lay down, and stopped crying. For another minute or so, William kept on "talking" while Jackson fell asleep. Once Jackson was asleep in his crib, William abruptly stopped talking, slowly lowered himself down into his crib, and fell asleep. I was truly amazed. William wanted to sleep. I don't know what he said to Jackson, but whatever it was, he certainly solved his problem.

— Jill Getto Lee, RIE Associate

Caring for multiples can be especially tiring, so steal some rest whenever you can. Friends and family may want to lend a hand but may not know what you really need. Make a list of ways they can support you, and don't be shy about asking for help. In the early weeks, having someone prepare a meal, run an errand, do the laundry, or hold a baby can make an enormous difference.

SIBLING CONFLICT

It may take a while for your toddler to learn that, unlike his doll that he can squeeze tightly, his baby sister doesn't like this and needs to be touched gently and hugged without being squished. It is up to the parent to ensure the safety of both children and to protect the baby from an aggressive or enthusiastic older sibling. If your toddler pokes or strikes out at his baby sister, in anger or just to see how she responds, of course, you have to intervene. Whenever possible, see if the children can resolve a conflict on their own, and when mediation is necessary, do your best to model peaceful conflict resolution without taking sides.

RIE definitely helped me to wait and observe any sibling disagreements before just jumping in. It gave me faith that they really could work it out on their own. As is often the case between kids, siblings or not, some things seemed to resolve very easily. For example, it didn't really matter to my younger son that the older one took something from him. Other times the older one really facilitated the resolution—sometimes with the help of only a little narration and other times completely on his own. I only really jump in if someone screams or asks for help. It's good to know that, often, intervening only creates problems where there are none, and it can even set a precedent for a cycle of one child (the baby) being treated like a victim.

—Dawnia Dresser

Just as we don't rush in to intervene in a conflict between two nonsiblings but instead wait to see what they can handle on their own, we also don't rush in to be the peacemaker or arbitrator between brother and sister. This is the beginning of a lifelong relationship, and like all relationships, it will have its struggles and disputes. Parents might hear an argument going on in the next room and go in to mediate. They haven't seen the beginning of the conflict and therefore can't accurately assess what really happened or what might be a fair resolution. It's always best not to assume the role of judge but instead to acknowledge the upset. "Keanu pushed you. You're upset." Sometimes a few empathic words are all that is needed. If the upset continues and your children are old enough, you may ask them to participate in finding a solution. When your older child grabs a play object from his baby sister, and the baby begins to wail, know that the baby's crying will stir something in her big brother. Rather than telling your older child to give it back, narrate what you see. Speak to the older child through his younger sister. "Mariana is crying and reaching for the ball. She's upset." Wait, then wait a little longer to see if your older child relinquishes the ball. If he doesn't, speak to Mariana. "You were playing with the ball, and now your brother has it. You're upset." This kind of language helps your older child hear and feel how his actions have affected his younger sister, and keeps you from being the judge and jury. Catch the moments when your older child is kind and gentle with his baby sister and comment on them. "Mariana is smiling. She looks so happy that you gave her the ball." As always, model the behavior you want to instill in your child and give him time to adapt and behave in a tolerant, if not loving, way with his sibling.

Our nine- and eleven-year-old boys have always shared a room. It's not a big space, and, of course, they occasionally have arguments over ownership of and playing with toys, but they're brief and infrequent. I attribute this to what our family learned at RIE. Narrating a recent situation and asking a question — "Truman, I see you have the cape and sword, and Sterling wants to play with it, too. How can you resolve this?" — diminishes the emotional charge inherent in the conflict. The threat of losing the toy, a turn, and worse, being misunderstood, is removed from the equation altogether. They decided — without my intervention — that the oven timer would be set, and each one of them would get the cape and sword for thirteen minutes apiece. The conflict usually dissolves into shared play because they have coestablished the rules of the game.

When it comes to these situations, our boys know that they don't have to fight for ownership of objects or of us.

— Diana Georger

For babies and toddlers, a new sibling or meeting unfamiliar people can come with a period of confusion and adaptation. Acknowledging these changes with honesty and sensitivity can help your child to feel seen and understood. When your baby experiences stranger anxiety, narrating can help to ease his upset. When a new baby is born, reassure him that his new sibling has not replaced him in your affection. Communicating openly with your child from the beginning of life will not only ease his distress in the moment but serve him well throughout his life.

10. Child Care

Infants need to believe that they are loved because of who they are. We need sensitive caregivers who can communicate that.

—Magda Gerber, *Dear Parent*

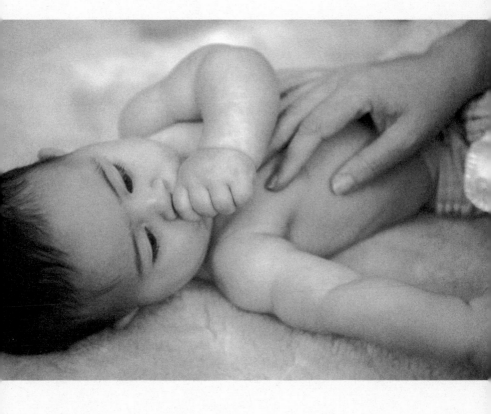

Magda believed that it was ideal for one parent to be home to take care of the children, even if sacrifices were necessary to make this happen. Unfortunately, this is financially impossible for most families today. How do you go about finding the best possible caregiving situation for your baby, and what do you look for? Some babies are cared for by a grandparent or other relative or an in-home caregiver or nanny; others attend day care or a child care center. There is no right solution for all families and all situations. What is important is the *quality* of the care that your baby will receive.

If you are looking for someone to care for your baby in your own home, start by looking for a caregiver who is peaceful and kind and who naturally moves slowly. A friendly, bubbly, energetic person might be just the right match for your four-year-old, but will she be able to slow herself down sufficiently to care for your baby? Ask the caregiver about her own upbringing to see what that reveals. If her childhood was a happy one, that's obviously a positive sign.

You can't get to know someone well during the course of a brief meeting, of course, but during an initial interview, you can ask a few questions that will help you understand whether or not this person's style is compatible with your own. "How would you put my baby down for a nap?" "What if she cries after you've put her down? How would you respond?" "If you're feeding her and she hasn't eaten all her food, what would you do?" "If my toddler takes an object from another child, how would you respond?" If the caregiver's response indicates a style different from your own, you might say, "As soon as my baby turns her head away from the food, closes her lips, or pushes the spoon away, I know that she's done eating. Sometimes she eats a lot and sometimes a little. Do you think you'd be comfortable looking for her cues and letting her decide?" There are few caregivers who have RIE experience, and that's okay. By having a conversation together, you may be able to find out if this person is open to another way of seeing babies and caring for them, or if she's more set in her ways. Can you imagine this person fitting in easily with your family and, more important, with your baby?

In most cases, it's much easier to communicate your expectations to an in-home caregiver than to a relative, with whom you have a history and ongoing relationship. But very often, having a relative care for your baby is less expensive or free, so it may be your best or only option. It's important to anticipate things beforehand and discuss issues that are important to you. It might be challenging to tell your mother-in-law that you prefer her to pick your baby up this way rather than that, or request that she stop handing play objects to her. How will you handle it if she swoops your baby up when she falls or distracts her during a diaper change? Rather than wait until you're in the thick of it, talk about these things in advance. Your baby may be able to tolerate a small amount of time with someone who has an entirely different style from yours, but many hours may be stressful for her.

It may be impossible to suggest things to a caregiver who works in a child care center that already has an established style and way of doing things, but when someone is caring for your baby in your home, you can certainly help your caregiver to follow RIE principles. If you want her to implement the Educaring Approach, it won't be possible for her to also be your housekeeper or perform other tasks. She can tidy up the kitchen or put in a load of wash while your baby is sleeping, but if her primary job is to care for your child, explain that you want her to devote her time and attention to your baby. Let her know that when it's time for uninterrupted play, she doesn't need to entertain your baby or be her playmate but can sit quietly nearby and observe her as she plays and be available to her when needed. You might ask her to notice what object your baby plays with and what she does with it and report back to you. She can tell you verbally or jot down a few notes to share with you at the end of the day. In this way, you can help your caregiver develop her observation skills and notice how much your baby is doing on her own. Let her know that when your baby cries, it's all right to slow down and wait before rushing in. It will be useful and informative for both of you to spend time together with your baby before your caregiver begins caring for your baby on her own, so that she can see your style and so there is the opportunity for conversation. This warming-in period gives your caregiver time to get used to you, your baby, your home, and your approach and gives your baby time to become accustomed to her new caregiver. By giving time, the transition will be easier for everyone.

CHILD CARE CENTERS

If you're considering family child care, home day care, or a child care center, do as much research as you can ahead of time. Call several centers to see if you can arrange a time to visit, and ask if you can spend an hour or so observing the babies in the room where your child would be. See if when you visit, the director will be available to answer a few questions such as these:

- Does the center have primary caregiving, where one caregiver is responsible for her own small group of babies, whom she diapers, feeds, and puts in their cribs to rest?

Primary caregiving is important because it affords the baby the opportunity to build an attachment to one significant person. This primary caregiver can be supported by others with whom your baby can become familiar, but it's important that each adult's role be clearly defined. It is not ideal for babies to be cared for by an ever-changing cast of characters, nor is it in your baby's best interest to be cared for by students or interns who are "practicing" with your baby.

- What is the caregiver-to-child ratio?

It's best if one adult is responsible for caring for no more than four children. It's not possible to give attentive care to a large number of babies at one time.

- How many children are in each room?

Small groups of babies—four is ideal, but no more than six—should be in each room. When a lot of babies are in one room, even if the adult-to-child ratio is small, it is impossible for the environment to be intimate and peaceful because of all of the hubbub.

- How are the groups of babies organized?

It's ideal for the groups to consist of babies who are within a few months in age and of like gross motor stages, so that the children are free to move and explore. When babies who are not yet crawling are put in the same room with toddlers, the babies can't relax because there are toddlers moving quickly around them, and the toddlers need to be restricted from moving freely to protect the babies. It's also challenging to provide an environment that is appropriate for mixed ages without sacrificing somewhere. Mixed-age groups can work beautifully for nursery-school-age children who are all walking and running, but not for babies and toddlers.

- Will your child stay together with her peer group when she reaches a certain age or developmental milestone?

Although a group of three-month-old babies may all start off on their backs, they won't all progress through their developmental stages at exactly the same pace. Some may begin to crawl weeks before others, and one baby may begin to walk months earlier than the rest. Your baby has formed relationships with her caregiver and the other babies in the group; they have become her family away from home. It will be preferable for your baby to stay with the same group throughout her tenure at the child care center rather than being moved to a new group when she begins to crawl or toddle or when she reaches a certain age. There may be a few weeks or months when one baby is still crawling and the others are all toddling; caregivers can manage this easily because all the babies are moving, with the ability to move away from one another if they choose to do so.

- Does the same caregiver stay with your baby as she transitions from one room to another?

If young babies start off at a center in the young infant room and are then transitioned to an older infant room and eventually a toddler room, it's ideal for the caregiver to move along with the children rather than the children having to transition to a new set of caregivers in each new room. This is called *continuity of care*.

- Is there an outdoor play area?

Having the opportunity to spend time outdoors, for babies to watch the clouds roll by and for toddlers to run and climb, is very important for emotional and physical well-being. Find out how often the children are able to go outside, and see if the outdoor space is accessible by the children, so that they can crawl or walk in and out as they please. Spending time outdoors in a stroller or taking a walk is very different from having the opportunity for outdoor uninterrupted play.

Before any of these questions are answered, you can get a feeling about a center as soon as you walk in the door. Does it feel peaceful and pleasant, or is there a din? Do the adults speak in quiet voices, or do they talk to one another and the children from across the room? Is there a safe space for your baby to play peacefully on her own? Are the play objects passive or active and noisy? Do the children seem engaged in their play? Content, happy? Is the caregiver paying attention and enjoying being with the babies, or is she daydreaming or talking to another caregiver? Do the adults let the babies play quietly, or do they interrupt them with needless comments? If a baby cries, how does the caregiver react? If you see a diaper change, does the caregiver talk to the baby, or does she offer an object to distract the baby? These are all things to look for, but also remember that taking care of several babies all day long is a very difficult job, and no center is perfect. If you get a warm feeling when you're observing and feel that the people who work there care about the babies and enjoy what they do, that's very positive. Look critically but understand that it will be impossible to find any place that you can't find some fault in.

I was so fortunate that my first real experience working in child care was in a center that was heavily RIE influenced. I didn't realize it at the time; I didn't even know what RIE was, but I knew that I was very happy with my job and felt peaceful... which I did not expect when I signed up to work in a room full of infants! Though the center had twelve infants to a room, we used primary caregiving, and I discovered the value of developing deep, caring connections with each of the three children on my team and their parents.

Certainly there were times when many, or even all, of the babies cried at once, but the tenor of a room full of crying babies is very different when all the caregivers are calm, peaceful, and understanding.

Working in such a center took me a little outside my comfort zone at first. I was encouraged to simply sit back and observe a child struggle to climb up a structure, which was hard... I really wanted to help! But I was shown how to observe the difference between a child struggling and succeeding and one who was struggling and looking for help. When a child cried, I was counseled not to rush but to approach slowly and calmly...to avoid saying, "It's okay," or distracting or teasing her tears away. I was encouraged to sit back and watch children play more often than taking time to lead children in play. And I was always, always to tell a child before I picked her up and to talk with her about what I was doing. Some of these things were easier to get used to than others, but I think that these little habits taught me to slow down, observe, and really look for children's capabilities, which helped me see them as individuals.

I vividly remember the shock of running into a family out doing some Christmas shopping at the mall. I remembered being so surprised to see their daughter Ann look so, well, like an infant! She was tucked into a stroller, and in the middle of a bustling mall, she looked rather small and defenseless. It made me realize what a gift it was to get to know her in an environment that was truly designed for her: I'd gotten used to seeing her as fully capable and autonomous.

— Melani Ladygo, RIE Associate

TRANSITIONING TO A NEW CAREGIVER

Another important consideration is how to help your baby become accustomed to a new caregiver. Your baby has a relationship with you, and even if her new caregiver is kind and gentle, in the beginning, she or he will be a stranger to your baby. Plan ahead so that your baby has plenty of time to get to know this new person, warm to him or her, and form a bond before you leave for an extended time. How long the transition takes and how easily or successfully it happens will depend on your baby's age and temperament. The transition will be more difficult and will likely take more time if your baby is experiencing separation or stranger anxiety. Whether your baby will be cared for in your home or at a center, it's ideal if you can begin the transition process *at least* two weeks before you go back to work. If a center offers home visits, that's a wonderful opportunity for you and your baby to begin to get to know the caregiver in your home before your baby spends time at the center. If the center does not offer home visits, ask about its transition process. It's ideal if you can spend time with your baby at the center for at least a couple of weeks. This will help both of you get to know your baby's caregiver and other staff members, and to feel at ease in the new environment. If someone will be caring for your baby in your home, have your caregiver start work at least two weeks before you return to work. Begin by spending time with the caregiver each day until you see that she is comfortable caring for your baby and that your baby is comfortable with this new person. Invite the caregiver to stand next to the changing table while you diaper your baby, and to sit quietly nearby when you feed her. Whether at a center or in your home, once you see that your baby is comfortable with her caregiver, spend some time out of the room, leaving her with her caregiver. Start by leaving for just a minute or two. Remember to tell your baby that you are leaving and will come back in two minutes, and make sure she sees you and knows when you return. If she's involved with a play object, get down on her level and let her know you've come back. When your baby is comfortable without you there for two minutes, gradually extend your time away so that you are out of the room for five minutes, then ten, fifteen, thirty; then an hour, two, and longer. Giving everyone time to get to know each other and for your baby to form a bond with her new caregiver is respectful and sets the stage for success.

No matter what type of child care you choose—whether it's in your home or at a center—take the time to build a relationship with your baby's caregiver(s). As your baby grows and her needs change, everyone involved in her care should feel free to ask questions and make suggestions to ensure that everyone is on the same page and your baby is well cared for.

11. Parenting Support

Parents may need others with whom they can commiserate on the fears and share the joys and hopes, the ups and downs of parenthood and infancy.

—Magda Gerber, *Dear Parent*

Working parents may look forward to the weekend, when they can spend all day with their baby. Stay-at-home parents may be eager for some time away, when they can get out of the house or apartment and be on their own or with a friend. Caring for a baby is a physically and emotionally difficult job. No one can do it well without a break from time to time. My sister Cindy, who raised four children and was a stay-at-home mother for several years, always looked forward to her daily run, even in the dead of winter. Just knowing there is someone to relieve you so that you can go for a thirty-minute walk in the neighborhood each day can be enormous. Magda used to ask parents at the end of each class, "What will you do for yourself this week?"

It can bring comfort and relief to talk to other parents about their trials and tribulations, share stories and ideas, and have a few laughs. You may want to organize a small group of parents who have babies of a similar age to get together weekly; three or four families may be ideal, and six or seven is probably too many. The group can meet at your or another person's home, although it's preferable to meet in the same home each week so that the babies can become familiar with the space. Having a backup location for weeks when you (or your baby) are sick may be a good idea. Wherever you meet, it's important that the space be completely childproofed so that everyone can sit back, relax, and enjoy being together without having to hop up and down to rescue a baby from a potential danger.

Although play objects can peacefully be passed from one

young baby to another, toddlers can have difficulty sharing their precious play objects with other children, especially at home. Having a separate set of objects that are used only by the group can help to avoid potential conflicts. When the babies are young, ask each parent to bring two or three objects from home for the babies to play with each week—and take them home afterward to be washed and ready for the following week. With toddlers, each parent in the group can find three or four play objects to contribute to the communal collection. These objects will be used only when the group gets together and will be put away at the end of each meeting. Remember, you don't need a lot of play objects, and many of them can be found in your kitchen.

Establishing some structure will help your group to be successful. A few guidelines will allow you to enjoy each other's company without things falling apart because you were paying too little attention to the babies. You'll want to set a regular time to meet, one that accommodates various sleeping schedules. Midday is often a time when young babies are awake, and once the babies are down to one nap a day, early morning or late afternoon meetings are often preferable. I would suggest that you set an end time for your meeting and stick to it. Sometimes parents are having so much fun being together that they lose track of the fact that their babies tired twenty minutes earlier. To make the group a positive experience for all, try to say your good-byes before the babies are overtired. How long should you meet? RIE Parent-Infant Guidance classes are ninety minutes. This is sometimes a little too long for a very young baby and too short for a toddler. As you observe your child, you'll see when he's tired. If the meeting is in your home and your baby is done, you may want to quietly disappear to feed him or lay him down for a rest.

I suggest that you encourage the parents to enter your home quietly. If you can leave the door unlocked so they can just come in when they get there, so much the better. Let them know where they can leave their diaper bags and their shoes— your safe play space is a no-shoes area, remember? If they haven't been to your home before, show them where the bathroom is. If you have enough room for people to nurse or bottle feed in a separate area from the play space, show that to them, too. Familiarizing everyone with your home before they sit down in the play space with their babies will prevent the necessity of a lot of getting up and down.

You may want to lay down a few simple guidelines before your first meeting. Ask parents to enter the play space and sit down quietly when they first arrive. Talking softly and moving slowly are also good places to start. Perhaps the first fifteen or twenty minutes of your get-together can be a time for quiet observation. This will help the parents keep their focus on the babies and will help the babies transition to being together. Once this observation period has ended, you can talk about what you noticed and just enjoy being together. If a parent is struggling with something she'd like support on, it can be comforting to know that other parents in the room may be struggling with much the same issue. Parents in my classes have given valuable advice on introducing new foods and how to prepare them. They've commiserated about sleep issues and dealing with their toddlers' strong points of view. They've offered emotional support and reassurance just when it was needed. Getting together with other parents can help you find answers to your questions and can be just plain fun.

The first sentence of *Baby Knows Best* is "Parenting is a difficult job and one that is impossible to fully prepare for." Whether your new baby is your first child or your fourth, raising a child is often challenging and always changing. It can be comforting to learn that other parents have many of the same questions that you have, and a relief and pleasure to get together with other parents to share stories, experiences, and ideas.

Afterword

On the last day of RIE Foundations courses, Magda Gerber asked her students, "If you had one wish, what would it be?" On the last day of my course, Magda visited and asked her famous question. Several people talked about their desire for world peace and happy babies and families. I was stumped by having to choose just one wish and contemplated my answer as if the fate of the world depended on it. Now, all these years later, I find myself thinking about my one wish for this book about Magda's work. It is this: I wish that this book shows you a path to an easier and more pleasurable life with your baby, one based on mutual trust and respect for each other.

In RIE Parent-Infant Guidance classes, I have been fortunate to see how people of diverse backgrounds and beliefs are able to implement Magda's principles. Over time and with practice, the Educaring Approach helps mothers and fathers bring new awareness to their parenting. They are able to see their babies as if through a new lens, one that reveals their baby's sometimes surprising levels of competency and his or her authentic self. I've been humbled by parents who openly share their struggles. I've been awed by tender interactions between parents and their babies. I've been moved to tears by a gentle touch, a kind word, a patient hand. These small but significant gestures convey the love we have for our children. These, then—more than shiny toys or exciting adventures— form our *relationship* with our child. And that is what truly matters.

Acknowledgments

Thank you to Magda Gerber, whose book *Your Self-Confident Baby* changed my life as a parent and a professional. I am grateful to Dr. Emmi Pikler, a visionary thinker who encouraged us to see babies as competent human beings from the beginning of their lives.

Thank you to my RIE teachers and mentors, who continue to inspire me: my first RIE teacher, Elizabeth Memel, whose weekly Parent-Infant Guidance classes stimulated and upended my thinking about babies and parenting and inspired me to learn more; my RIE Foundations instructor, Beverly Kovach, in whose class I discovered that Magda's work fascinated me, even without my son in the room; and my Practicum Mentor Teacher, Carol Pinto, who embodies the Educaring Approach in her wise and gentle ways.

Deep thanks and appreciation go to my RIE colleague Melani Ladygo, who offered invaluable support with research and gave her usual thoughtful input on the manuscript, all done with her keen Educaring eye and attention to detail.

Thanks and appreciation to my RIE colleagues who read and commented on early drafts of the manuscript: Deborah Greenwald, whose thoughtful queries make me a more sensitive Educarer; Ruth Anne Hammond, who wrestled controversial RIE questions with me; Elizabeth Memel, who helped me to refine and clarify my ideas; and Carol Pinto, who carefully considered even the smallest details.

Thank you to my RIE colleague Alexandra Curtis Boyer who generously shared her gross motor development paper with me and also directed me to research that had been elusive.

Thanks also to Feldenkrais practitioner Beth Rubenstein, MS, PT, who provided unique insight on gross motor development issues.

My endless gratitude goes to Barrow Davis-Tolot for the beautiful photographs on the cover and throughout the book. We laugh now about how I naively e-mailed her two months before the manuscript was due to see if she wanted to "take some photos for the book." Little did I know what was involved, but Barrow took on the job with her usual enthusiasm and gusto. She not only art directed and took stunning photos but acted as photo editor as well, sifting through thousands of photos to distill them down to what you see here.

Thank you to the parents who so generously let us photograph them and their babies in Parent-Infant Guidance classes and in their homes, and to everyone who contributed RIE stories and quotes for the book.

Thank you to RIE's literary agent, Meg Thompson at Einstein Thompson Agency, for suggesting that it might be time for a new book about the Educaring Approach and for her thoughtful guidance along the way.

To Harriet Bell, I extend my enduring gratitude and profound thanks for her patient, kind, and artful hand throughout the writing process. Harriet always managed to gently ask the right question or wisely offer a suggestion to get me unstuck, all with abundant good humor.

Thank you to Tracy Behar, my editor at Little, Brown, for her creative and skilled expertise in crafting this book and for her generous way of demystifying the publishing process. It has been a fascinating journey.

Thank you to Magda Gerber's children, Daisy Gerber, Mayo Gerber Nagy, and Bence Gerber. It is an honor to teach parents and caregivers about your mother's respectful approach to being with babies.

Thank you to RIE President Polly Elam and to the RIE Board of Directors for entrusting me with the writing of this book and giving me the time to write it. A special thanks to board member Mendes Napoli for his wise counsel and support.

To members of the RIE Alliance of Associates everywhere, thank you for generously sharing Magda's Educaring Approach with others and, in so doing, improving the lives of babies and their families.

Thank you to all the mothers and fathers who have brought their babies to Parent-Infant Guidance classes and from whom I have learned so much.

Thank you to all the caregivers who practice the Educaring Approach in their daily lives with babies and young children. You are true angels.

Thank you to Richard Carr, whose guidance over the years has made me a better parent, teacher, and person.

Thank you to my mother, Nancy Higley, for her enduring optimism and support, during this project and always.

Finally, thank you to my husband, Jonny Solomon, who has always been an enthusiastic partner on our parenting journey and who made it possible for me to write this book. He cleared the way so that I would have time to write without interruption, and silently served me food when I dared not leave the computer. I could not have done it without him. And to my son, Elijah, who changed my life for the better and without whom I might never have discovered Magda Gerber.

Resources

Many parents ask where they can purchase equipment for use at home. Gates and enclosures are the only required, "must have it" items. The other pieces of equipment may be something that friends or family members can contribute to as a baby gift.

Feeding Equipment

http://www.duralexusa.com/Picardie-Tumbler-Clear-3-1-ounce
-Set-of-6-plu1023AB06/6.html

Foam Mats

http://www.wondermat.com
http://www.softtiles.com

Gates and Enclosures

http://www.rightstart.com/search/result/index/?limit=all&ocat=356

Toddler Gross Motor Equipment

Note: You may see some gross motor equipment that is carpeted, but this is unnecessary. Plain wooden equipment is most preferable.

Stairs

http://www.communityplaythings.com/products/ridingtoys/V43.html
http://www.sensoryedge.com/redrocker.html

Step and ramp

http://www.whitneybros.com/product-catalog/20

Tunnels

http://www.communityplaythings.com/products/communityloft/
nurserygym/index.html

http://www.whitneybros.com/infant-toddler-play/toddler-play/toddler
-low-ground-tunnel

DVDs and CDs

Beatty, T., and C. Stranger. *Seeing Infants with New Eyes*. DVD.
Resources for Infant Educarers, 1984. Available from http://
www.rie.org/categories/dvd.

Beatty, T., and C. Stranger. *Viendo al bebé con nuevos ojos* [Seeing Infants
with New Eyes]. DVD. Resources for Infant Educarers, 1984.
Available from http://www.rie.org/categories/dvd.

Gerber, M., and R. Christianson. *Mira comó se mueven* [See How They
Move]. DVD. Resources for Infant Educarers, 1989. Available
from http://www.rie.org/categories/dvd.

Gerber, M., and R. Christianson. *See How They Move*. DVD.
Resources for Infant Educarers, 1989. Available from http://
www.rie.org/categories/dvd.

Resources for Infant Educarers. *Magda Gerber's Educaring® Approach:
An Audio Guide for Nurturing Nannies and Other Caregivers*. CD in
English and Spanish. Resources for Infant Educarers, 2011.
Available from http://www.rie.org/categories/dvd.

Resources for Infant Educarers. *RIE® Conference DVDs*. Resources for
Infant Educarers, 2010–13. Available from http://www.rie.org/
categories/dvd.

Resources for Infant Educarers and J. Solomon. *See How They Play*.
DVD. Resources for Infant Educarers, 2013. Available from
http://www.rie.org/categories/dvd.

Books

By Magda Gerber

Dear Parent: Caring for Infants with Respect. Los Angeles: Resources for
Infant Educarers, 1998. http://www.rie.org/product/dear-parent.

The RIE Manual for Parents and Professionals, Expanded Edition. Magda
Gerber and Deborah Greenwald, eds. Los Angeles: Resources
for Infant Educarers, 2013. http://www.rie.org/product/the-rie
-manual.

Your Self-Confident Baby. By Magda Gerber and Allison Johnson. New York: John Wiley and Sons, 1998. http://www.rie.org/product/ your-self-confident-baby-how-to-encourage-your-child's-natural -abilities-from-the-very-start.

By Other Authors

Boyer, Alexandra Curtis. *Simple Toys Make Active Babies*. Available from the RIE website. English version: http://www.rie.org/product/ simple-toys-make-active-babies. Spanish version: http://www.rie .org/product/juguetes-simple-hacen-bebes-activos.

Hammond, Ruth Anne. *Respecting Babies: A New Look at Magda Gerber's RIE Approach*. Zero to Three, 2009. http://www.rie.org/ product/respecting-babies.

Kovach, Beverly, and Denise Da Ros-Voseles. *Being with Babies: Understanding and Responding to the Infants in Your Care*. Gryphon House, 2008. http://www.rie.org/product/being-with-babies.

Kovach, Beverly, and Susan Patrick. *Being with Infants and Toddlers: A Curriculum That Works for Caregivers*. LBK Publishing, 2012. http://www.rie.org/product/being-with-toddlers.

Petrie, Stephanie, and Sue Owen, eds. *Authentic Relationships in Group Care for Infants and Toddlers — Resources for Infant Educarers (RIE): Principles into Practice*. London: Jessica Kingsley, 2005. http://www .rie.org/product/authentic-relationships.

Pikler Institute. *Unfolding of Infants' Natural Gross Motor Development*. Resources for Infant Educarers, 2006. http://www.rie.org/ product/unfolding.

Roche, Mary Alice, ed. *Emmi Pikler, 1902–1984*. Sensory Awareness Foundation Bulletin 14, Winter 1994. Mill Valley, CA: Sensory Awareness Foundation. http://www.rie.org/product/pikler -bulletin-14.

Vander Zande, Irene. *1, 2, 3 . . . The Toddler Years*. Santa Cruz, CA: Santa Cruz Toddler Care Center, 1995. http://www.rie.org/ product/1-2-3-the-toddler-years.

More about RIE

**RESOURCES
FOR INFANT
EDUCARERS**

Resources for Infant Educarers (RIE) was founded in 1978 by infant specialist and educator Magda Gerber and pediatric neurologist Tom Forrest, M.D. RIE is an international, non-profit organization dedicated to improving the quality of infant care and education around the globe. Teaching, supporting, and mentoring parents and professionals, RIE offers a variety of classes, workshops, conferences, and mentoring opportunities that support adults and babies in their lives together.

Visit the RIE website:
http://www.rie.org

Become an RIE member:
http://www.rie.org/membership

Learn about RIE Parent-Infant Guidance classes:
http://www.rie.org/classes/parent-infant

Learn about RIE Professional Development courses:
http://www.rie.org/classes/profdevel

Learn about the RIE Alliance and its members:
http://rie.org/alliance

Make a donation to RIE:
http://www.rie.org/donate

Browse RIE-related blogs and websites:
http://www.deborahcarlislesolomon.com
http://www.janetlansbury.com
http://www.magdagerber.org
http://www.regardingbaby.org

Notes

Introduction

1. Magda Gerber and Allison Johnson, *Your Self-Confident Baby*
   (New York: John Wiley and Sons, 1998), xv–xvi.

Chapter One: The RIE Way

1. Gerber, *Dear Parent*, 1.
2. Gerber, *Dear Parent*, 11.
3. Gerber, *Dear Parent*, 159.
4. Gerber, *Dear Parent*, 67.
5. Gerber, *Dear Parent*, 183.
6. Gerber, *Dear Parent*, 5.
7. Gerber, *Dear Parent*, 63.
8. Gerber, *Dear Parent*, 107–8.
9. Mary Alice Roche, ed., *Sensory Awareness Foundation Bulletin*
   14, Winter 1994 (Mill Valley, CA: Sensory Awareness Foundation,
   1994), 21.
10. Arietta Slade, "Parental Reflective Functioning: An Introduction,"
    Attachment and Human Development 7, no. 3 (September 2005):
    269–81.

Chapter Two: At Home with Your Newborn

1. Gerber and Johnson, *Your Self-Confident Baby*, 74.

Chapter Three: Caring for Your Baby

1. Carol Pinto, "Supporting Competence in a Child with Special
   Needs: One Child's Story," *Educaring Newsletter: Resources for
   Infant Educarers*, Spring 2001, 1, 5–6.

Chapter Four: Sleep

1. Gerber and Johnson, *Your Self-Confident Baby*, 38.
2. Douglas M. Teti, Bo-Ram Kim, Gail Mayer, and Molly Countermine, "Maternal Emotional Availability at Bedtime Predicts Infant Sleep Quality," *Journal of Family Psychology* 24, no. 3 (June 2010): 307–15, doi:10.1037/a0019306.
3. Melissa M. Burnham, Beth L. Goodlin-Jones, Erika E. Gaylor, and Thomas F. Anders, "Nighttime Sleep-Wake Patterns and Self-Soothing from Birth to One Year of Age: A Longitudinal Intervention Study," *Journal of Child Psychology and Psychiatry* 43, no. 6 (September 2002): 713–25, http://www.ncbi.nlm.nih.gov/pmc/articles/PMC1201415.
4. Marc Weissbluth, *Healthy Sleep Habits, Happy Child* (New York: Ballantine, 1999), 160.

Chapter Five: Free to Move

1. Gerber, *Dear Parent*, 153.
2. Pinto, "Supporting Competence in a Child with Special Needs."

Chapter Six: Play

1. Dimitri A. Christakis and Frederick J. Zimmerman, *The Elephant in the Living Room* (New York: Rodale, 2006), 26.
2. Council on Communications and Media, "Media Use by Children Younger than Two Years," *Pediatrics* 128, no. 5 (November 2011): 1040–45, doi:10.1542/peds.2011-1753.
3. The Pikler Institute, *Unfolding of Infants' Natural Gross Motor Development* (Los Angeles: Resources for Infant Educarers, 2006), 62.
4. E. Nagy and P. Molnar, "Heart Rate Deceleration During the Grasping Reflex," *European Journal of Pediatrics* 158, no. 7 (July 1999): 576–77.
5. Magda Gerber and Deborah Greenwald, eds., *The RIE Manual for Parents and Professionals, Expanded Edition* (Los Angeles: Resources for Infant Educarers, 2013), 158.
6. Gerber and Greenwald, *The RIE Manual for Parents and Professionals*, 158.

7. Alfie Kohn, "Five Reasons to Stop Saying Good Job," *Young Children*, Spring 2001.
8. Gerber, *Dear Parent*, 138.

Chapter Seven: Learning Limits

1. http://www.janetlansbury.com/2012/06/
   set-limits-without-yelling-more-toddler-discipline-mistakes.
2. Gerber, *Dear Parent*, 108.
3. Gerber, *Dear Parent*, 119.
4. Gerber and Johnson, *Your Self-Confident Baby*, 209.

Chapter Nine: As Your Baby and Family Grow

1. Gerber, *Dear Parent*, 123.
2. Shelly Vaziri Flais, *Raising Twins: From Pregnancy to Preschool* (American Academy of Pediatrics, 2010).

Index

About the Author

Deborah Carlisle Solomon is the executive director of RIE. She discovered RIE when her son was a baby, and was so deeply moved by the Educaring Approach that she decided to change careers to join the organization. She has addressed various national and international infancy and early-childhood conferences and workshops. She resides in Los Angeles with her husband and now RIE teenager, Elijah.